THE
LITTLE
HISTORY
OF
YORKSHIRE

THE
LITTLE
HISTORY
OF
YORKSHIRE

INGRID BARTON

First published 2018
Reprinted 2019

The History Press
The Mill, Brimscombe Port
Stroud, Gloucestershire, GL5 2QG
www.thehistorypress.co.uk

British Library Cataloguing in Publication Data.
A catalogue record for this book is available from the British Library.

ISBN 978 0 7509 8356 3

Typesetting and origination by The History Press
Printed and bound in Europe by Imak

CONTENTS

1

IN THE BEGINNING

In the beginning was the land.

To the west are the Pennines, a long hard backbone, wet and mountainous. The upper part is carboniferous limestone, heathland, shot through with veins of lead; the lower part peaty shale and millstone grit; boggy, difficult land.

To the north is a range of lower hills, uplands and dales, shaped by the glaciers of the last Ice Age, merging with the Pennines to the west. Here, in places, carboniferous limestone has dissolved to form characteristic swallow holes, or potholes like Gaping Gill. This block of hills is cut by the wide and fertile Eden Valley, on the further side of which it rises again as the Yorkshire Moors, taking its old name of Blackamoor from the peaty soil.

To the east rise the Wolds, an arc of chalk hills, made from the crushed bodies of countless trillions of sea creatures who once swam in a warm sea before the world we know was formed. This land is softer. The Ice Age rounded its hills and flattened the bottoms of its long-vanished becks.

Further East and South lies flat Holderness, once covered with meres (Hornsey Mere is the last), and straggling becks left by the Ice Age. It has always been a boggy land, liable to flooding, cut off from the rest of the country, but its alluvial soil is rich.

Framed on three sides by these ranges of hills is the easier, fertile land of the huge Vale of York and the smaller vales of Cleveland, Mowbray and Pickering. These are made richer with silt from the great rivers Ouse, Nidd, and Derwent. They were once vast wetlands covered in game and flocking birds. A band of magnesium limestone cut by the gorges of Knaresborough, Wharfe and Don overlooks the Vale of York.

When humans first settled in Yorkshire this was the land they had to survive on: some places easy and generous, some hard and meagre, some quirky, needing generations to learn to use.

In the beginning was the land, and the land brought forth the people!

YORKSHIRE FOLK:
The **Reverend Fred Kendall** is a forgotten early geologist, one of the founders of the Yorkshire Rotunda Museum. Expelled from Cambridge in 1817 for allegedly setting fire to his college (cleared at his trial) he went on to publish *A Catalogue of the Minerals and Fossils of Scarborough*, one of the pioneering works of geology.

PLACES TO VISIT:
Yorkshire is a feast for geologists where you will find rocks from many periods, such as:

   Robin Hood's Bay: Jurassic strata
   Flamborough Head: upper cretaceous chalk cliffs
   Nidd Gorge: dolomite limestone overlaid with gypsum
   Gaping Gill: a fine example of a limestone pot
   Rotunda Museum, Vernon Road, Scarborough, YO11 2PS

INTRODUCTION

Modern teaching of history is often too general to deal with the story of particular places, and yet that is precisely the sort of history to which people feel connected. Yorkshire has had a fabulous past and yet many Yorkshire people have little knowledge of it, which is why I wanted to write something for them.

Creating a little history of a county as big as Yorkshire was quite a challenge because so many important events happened here. Inevitably I have had to be selective, so I apologise if I've left out your favourite bit of Yorkshire history. What I *have* included is, at the end of each chapter, a paragraph about a particular Yorkshire person of the period, as well as a short list of relevant places that interested readers might like to visit.

My thanks go to my friends, Dr Charles Kightly (a *real* historian) who has very kindly corrected many of my mistakes, and Professor Pam King, who helped me with the Corpus Christi pageants. I'd also like to acknowledge my great obligation to Professor David Hey of Sheffield University, on whose really BIG history of Yorkshire I have modelled my own, and all those lovely people who created the hundreds of websites, helpful and otherwise, that I have consulted while writing this book.

Ingrid Barton,
Yorkshire, 2018

2

PREHISTORY

History is, technically, the study of evidence from written records, but humans were around in Yorkshire thousands of years before writing was invented. This 'before' time is called prehistory and relies on archaeological evidence. Prehistory was divided by Victorian archaeologists into three ages: the Stone, Bronze and Iron Ages, named after the commonest material for weapons and tools. These classifications, while still useful, are very rough. They vary depending on what resources were available to the people in any particular area and overlap in time a lot.

The Stone Age is also divided into three Ages: Old, Middle and New. The main material for tools in all three ages was flint, traded across Britain and Ireland. It was knapped with increasing skill over the years into artefacts often of great beauty. Actually, wood was probably the material in greatest use, but few artefacts survive.

OLD STONE AGE (PALEOLITHIC)

The first people to walk on the land we now call Yorkshire came here a very long time ago. It is hard for us to get our heads around the hundreds of thousands of years during which our ancestors lived hunting wild animals and gathering wild food. They were nomads, ranging over huge areas, exploiting seasonal sources of food. These early people came to Britain as visitors, not settlers.

The last Ice Age slowly drew to its conclusion at about 10,000 BC, but ice still covered the northern part of the country. At that time Britain was part of Europe, attached to the Netherlands, the west coast of Germany and Jutland by a low-lying area known to archaeologists as Doggerland: no English Channel, no North Sea. Doggerland was tundra, a good hunting country of mosses, lichens, marshes and bird-filled reedbeds over which small bands of hunter-gatherers occasionally crossed into southern Britain, and occasionally up into Yorkshire, though it was still very cold here. The animals they hunted were cold-weather ones: woolly mammoth, aurochs (a sort of giant bull), woolly rhinoceros, bison, elk and reindeer, some of which left their bones in Victoria Cave, near Settle. About 8,000 BC a hunter one day lost his harpoon point in a deer he had wounded; it died in Victoria Cave with the harpoon still in it and the skilfully-carved little tip is the first evidence of humans in Yorkshire.

MIDDLE STONE AGE (MESOLITHIC)

From about 10,000 BC big changes began to happen to Britain. As the climate warmed, the mosses and lichens on which the cold-weather animals fed began to be replaced by grass and trees, birch, alder and willow. While the ways from Europe were still open, the spread of grasslands enticed herds of different animals into Britain: deer, horses, wild cattle, wild pigs. However, as the ice melted Doggerland slowly began to flood and become impassable. The catastrophic collapse of a huge lake between England and Germany, in about 6,500 BC, scoured out the English Channel. From that time any humans and animals in Britain were effectually stranded. The Middle Stone Age covers this time of change, lasting from 10,000 to about 4,000 BC. Its most important archaeological site in Yorkshire – and probably in the whole country – is at Star Carr in North Yorkshire, where excavations carried out over many years have shed new light on the Mesolithic way of life.

Star Carr lies 5 miles south of Scarborough at the east end of the Vale of Pickering on the shores of a vanished lake, Lake Flixton. Dating from the time when Doggerland was still above water, this Mesolithic site was in a rich environment. Around the lake and along the wide Vale was an open mixed forest of birch, aspen and willow in which many animals lived. There were red and roe deer, wild horse, elk, aurochs, wild boar, wolves, lynx, pine marten and wildcat; beavers built dams in nearby becks; flocks of all sorts of birds flew among the water lilies, reeds and edible aquatic plants of the fish-filled lake; hares and hedgehogs hid in bushes on the shores; badgers trundled through the undergrowth. It was a perfect environment for humans to exploit.

It used to be thought that these hunter-gatherers did not build houses but lived in temporary camps; however, this is proving not to be the case. There was some sort of structure built on the shores of the lake, 3.5m wide, constructed of log posts, with an unknown infill, possibly skins. Its floor was covered with a thick layer of moss, reeds and soft plant material. While the building may possibly have been inhabited only seasonally it continued to be used for up to 500 years. There was also a trackway leading to a platform over the lake which may have been used for fishing.

The finds at Star Carr have been amazing. Large numbers of bone tools, flint scrapers and axes have been found as

well as the only engraved Mesolithic pendant in Britain. The most exciting finds are twenty-one deer skull frontlets which seem to relate to a deer cult. They are made from the top of skulls of red deer, with the antlers still attached. They are pierced with eyeholes so they were clearly intended for wearing, probably by shamans, during some hunting ceremony. Other items include rolls of birch bark and lumps of pyrites for lighting fires, and pieces of haematite for red paint.

NEW STONE AGE (NEOLITHIC)

There were comparatively few humans in existence any-where at the beginning of the Middle Stone Age but, few as they were, they were well on their way to becoming top predator. The disadvantage of being a hunter, however, is that hunting takes time, co-operation and energy. It can seldom supply enough food to support a large popula-tion. Gathering, too, takes time because plants are seasonal and have to be found. How much simpler to scatter the seeds near where you live! The people who first thought of scattering seeds in a convenient place took a huge step towards farming, which developed slowly from about 4,500 BC onwards. Having more food led to the invention of techniques for preserving it and so to increased survival in the winter months. Animals began to be domesticated and herded, with the new help of dogs; horses were tamed and ridden; simple ploughs were developed. Population numbers began to rise.

In Yorkshire, as in other parts of Britain, the larger population made it possible for communities to leave a lasting mark on the landscape. In the Wolds, where the lighter soils made clearing the land easier, communities worked together to mark some of their dead with the cigar-shaped mounds of chalk known as long barrows. Most have now been ploughed out, but the one excavated at Willerby Wold had a concave forecourt where burial rituals took place before the dead were laid in a wooden chamber. The whole thing was then covered with a chalk mound and burned.

Long barrows can be found all over Britain, but it's only in the Wolds that Neolithic round barrows can be found (much larger than the later ones from the Bronze Age). Willey and Duggleby Howes (from *haugr*, a Norse word for burial mound) stand impressively high above the road. Although quite a few people, including children, are interred in them, either as burials or cremations, we don't know why these particular people were chosen for the honour; most of the dead must have been disposed of in some other way.

Both howes are in the Great Wold Valley, the widest of the valleys that cut the Yorkshire Wolds. It contains the Gypsey Race, a mysteriously intermittent river which seems to have been the centre of a Neolithic sacred landscape. Duggleby Howe is surrounded by a recently discovered henge and further down the valley at a sharp bend in the Gypsey Race are the strange avenues of unknown use called cursuses as well as the massive Rudston Monument. This last is a huge standing stone some 8m high, cut from Jurassic grit-stone and dragged 28 miles from an outcrop at Grosmont. A row of similar stones called the Devil's Arrows stand outside Boroughbridge.

Henges are supposedly sacred circular spaces defined by a bank with an internal ditch. There are many, large and small, in Britain, but three of the most intriguing and impressive stand in a row near Thornborough, near Ripon, a place which seems to have been very important in the New Stone Age. If you stand on the northern bank the central henge seems irritatingly out of alignment with the other two, but recent computer analysis has revealed that the three henges are an exact match with the stars of Orion's Belt. Don't underestimate Neolithic astronomers!

There are many other important Neolithic features in Yorkshire. Henges can be found in the Pennines and there are at least a dozen long barrows on the North Yorkshire Moors. Rock art – small strange carvings and cup-and-ring markings – are being discovered all the time, some hidden on the undersides of rocks, some indicating droveways or paths across marshland, sometimes in full view overlooking a valley. Rombolds Moor, near Ilkley, has the best

collection of rock art in Yorkshire, but the interpretation of these signs is still in its infancy.

YORKSHIRE FOLK:
Born near Wetherby, **Augustus Pitt Rivers** became, during a successful military career, increasingly interested in archaeology and ethnology (the study of peoples). He believed that ordinary objects were important and collected a vast number of archaeological and ethnological items, ranging from shrunken heads to Eskimo trousers, which form the basis of the fascinating Pitt Rivers Museum in Oxford.

PLACES TO VISIT:
Victoria Cave: east of Langcliffe in Ribblesdale
Thornborough Rings: Thornborough, near Masham
Duggleby Howe: near village of Duggleby, Ryedale
The Rudston Monument: Rudston, East Riding of Yorkshire on the B1253 between Driffield and Bridlington

3

THE BRONZE AGE

Bronze is an alloy of copper and tin. At some time around 2,200 BC tools and weapons made of this material began to enter the country from the Continent. These could be sharpened more than flint and did not shatter, although they were easily blunted. Traders must have brought the first ones but copper was easy to find in Britain, and the secret of turning it into bronze was soon discovered. There are several bronze smelting sites from this age in Yorkshire.

Things crafted by a magical process into such a beautiful and powerful material – didn't it shine like the sun itself? – were very special. An axe with a socketed bronze head made you an important person and superior to those who continued to use flint. A tiny bronze axe-head pendent recently discovered in an excavation at Thixendale in the Wolds was probably a good luck charm, and there is evidence that many full-size bronze axe heads and spears were never used, but thrown into Yorkshire rivers as gifts for the gods. To the south of the county, in Holderness, a great range of bronze tools and weapons, probably offered in this way, have been found over the years.

In our county, as in other parts of Britain, it seems that the use of bronze was connected in some way with

increasing social divisions. There were still big communal projects, such as the building of huge dykes (banks with associated ditches) to mark tribal boundaries, but powerful people were now buried in their own mounds, accompanied by their most prized possessions and food for the afterlife placed in decorated pottery vessels.

In this period it is, once again, in the Yorkshire Wolds that the most important centres of population were located. The hills of the Wolds are covered with round Bronze Age burial mounds (smaller than the communal Neolithic ones), while dykes and earthworks show that the land continued to be divided up. Few actual settlements have yet been found, but a huge site at Paddock Hill, Thwing, shows what could be achieved. A deep outer ditch and chalk rampart 115m in diameter surrounded an internal ditch and very large round house, 25m across. In the centre of the house was a smaller ring of posts around a cremation, giving rise to the idea that the whole complex may have been a temple. However, as there is also evidence that bronze smelting, feasting, weaving and corn grinding went on there, it may have had some more everyday purpose.

In North Ferriby by the Humber, four log boats have been found. These are thought to be the oldest boats in

Europe and date from the early Bronze Age, about 4,000 years old. They are made of huge slabs of oak sewn together with twisted yew branches and were big enough to carry animals. It is not known whether they had masts or not, but recent experiments show that they were sturdy enough to have been used in coastal waters and even, perhaps, to cross the North Sea.

The North York Moors might not, nowadays, seem the best place to farm, but the climate was warmer in the past and the land more fertile; there is evidence for many small field enclosures in Eskdale and Upper Ryedale, marked by rubble walls and cairns of cleared stones. Those who farmed there left their important dead in the more than 200 burial mounds scattered over the area; some of them, like Lilla Howe, are prominent landmarks, well-loved by travellers heading towards Whitby. Most of the mounds contain only pottery food vessels, but a few people were buried with extra items, such as bronze daggers. One such was the so-called 'Gristhorpe Man', discovered in the 1830s at Gristhorpe near Scarborough. He was 6ft tall; a sign, possibly, of a superior diet, and died at a good age of natural causes, although he had a few healed fractures, consistent with his having been a warrior. He was wrapped in a skin cloak and laid in a hollowed tree trunk. Buried with him were a bronze dagger, a bark vessel, flint tools, and a wicker basket containing food residue.

Population increase in Bronze Age Yorkshire seems to have led to disputes over access to resources. This inevitably resulted in the increased demarcation of the land. Lines of howes across the horizon, or increased building of dykes warned neighbouring groups whose territory they were entering. Some of these dykes, probably major tribal boundaries, are huge with multiple banks, like the Scamridge Dykes. Some, such as those in the Hambledon and Tabular Hills, enclose areas that include all the different types of land necessary for successful farming: grazing, arable and meadow land.

YORKSHIRE FOLK:

Ted Wright and his brother Will were teenagers in 1937 when they discovered the remains of a Bronze Age boat in North Ferriby on the Humber foreshore. Ted had found two more by 1963. All of the same type, they would have been 16m long and were built of oak planks sewn together with yew withies. 'Ferriby 3' was dated to 1900 BC, making it the oldest sewn-plank boat in Europe.

PLACES TO VISIT:

Cockmore Dykes: These massive boundary dykes can be viewed from the adjacent National Park car park

Scamridge Dykes

Bronze Age rock art can be found in many places on the West Yorkshire moors. See the 'Elephant's Eye' stone among others on Ilkley Moor

The Hull and East Riding Museum: Featuring Bronze Age food vessels and a model of the Thwing temple. Entrance free

4

THE IRON AGE

Theoretically the Iron Age dates from the first introduction of iron to Britain, in around 700 BC, up until the Roman invasion. In fact, life for most folk went on in much the same way as it had for hundreds of years before. Archaeological evidence from Staple Howe farm, Knapton and elsewhere show that family groups lived, as their ancestors had, in large round houses made of wood or stone with thatched roofs. Pigs wandered and rooted around them. They cultivated small arable plots of barley, spelt and emmer wheat and grazed herds of small sturdy sheep, cattle and horses on high ground in summer, driving them down to lower ground in winter, as farmers still do in the Lake District. Trade, however, inevitably brings change and things were altering slowly as new ideas, fashions and people filtered into the country from abroad; above all there were the exciting possibilities of this new metal: iron.

Iron was not as beautiful as bronze, but it was stronger and kept its edge better, which was ideal for weapons. Warriors quickly took to it but, just as in the Bronze Age, it was initially only those at the top of society who possessed iron objects. Gradually techniques for smelting

iron were learned and sources of iron-rich stone discovered, though in Yorkshire bog iron – impure iron deposits that develop in swampy areas – was sometimes used, notably in Nidderdale and the River Foulness area near Market Weighton.

Aerial photography has revealed that much more of Yorkshire was farmed in the Iron Age than appears on the ground. Extensive hut circles, field boundaries and ladder settlements (where houses and fields are connected together in straight lines like ladders) can be seen as crop marks in many places. The Wolds were, it seems, once again more heavily populated than the rest of Yorkshire. Early ploughs could cope better with the light Wold soils than the heavier clays of the Vale of York. New land was brought into cultivation as the population increased, and the system of Bronze Age dykes was greatly extended as land was divided more and more.

It is in the Iron Age that we first hear the names of local tribes, thanks to Roman writers such as Ptolemy. The most important were the Brigantes, whose name means something like 'The High Ones'. The precise boundaries of their territory are uncertain but they spread right across most of what is now Yorkshire, probably as far south as the Don. It is now thought that their tribal capital was at Stanwick, north of Richmond, where there is a huge complex of ramparts and buildings like a town. In its day it must have been very impressive, a place to which traders brought exotic Roman goods such as Samian pottery, wine and glass.

Demonstrating power as a warlord seems to have been a particular feature of the Iron Age throughout Britain. Hillforts were the must-have items for every petty kinglet. The highest in Yorkshire (and England) is on the cold, windswept, waterless top of Ingleborough, where its benighted inhabitants lived in twenty round houses. Other more accessible Brigantian hillforts can be found at Castle Hill, Almondbury, Brierley Common and Bolton Scar on the moors. Recognised only in 2001, the huge hillfort at Roulston Scar near Sutton Bank has walls nearly 8ft high.

The other Iron Age tribe in Yorkshire was that of the Parisi, who lived in what is now East Yorkshire. Possibly related to the Parisii tribe who founded Paris, they differed from other British tribes in that they buried their adult dead in barrows surrounded by square ditches with rounded corners (children were buried in ordinary graves nearby). Joints of pork as well as personal possessions often accompanied the dead. Huge cemeteries containing hundreds of these barrows in all sizes have been found on the slopes of the Wolds. The site called 'Danes' Graves' near Driffield is a still visible example.

So far twenty of these graves have been found to contain dismantled two-wheeled 'chariots' and, unexpectedly, a number of their deceased owners were women. These vehicles were probably not war chariots but light swift carts. Only two have ever been found outside Parisi territory, one in Scotland and one near Ferrybridge, where there is evidence of a particularly lavish funeral feast including some 250 cattle. Quite a party!

YORKSHIRE FOLK:

John Robert Mortimer (15 June 1825–19 August 1911) was an archaeologist living in Driffield who was responsible for excavating most of the main burial mounds in the Yorkshire Wolds, publishing his findings in his snappily-titled book *Forty Years Researches in British and Saxon Burial Mounds of East Yorkshire*. The museum of archaeology that he established in Driffield was one of the earliest of its kind and he was one of the first archaeologists to apply scientific methods to archaeology.

PLACES TO VISIT:

The Hull and East Riding Museum: Iron Age (Celtic) exhibition with reconstruction of a chariot. Open 10 a.m.–5 p.m. Monday to Saturday and 1.30–4.30 p.m. on Sunday. Entrance free

Castle Hill: Iron Age fort in Almondbury overlooking Huddersfield West Yorkshire

Wincobank Hill Fort: near Sheffield. Thought to have been built by the Brigantes

5

THE ROMANS

Julius Caesar invaded Britain in 55 BC but the Romans did nothing more until AD 43 when the Emperor Claudius, ostensibly at the request of a British king, landed near what is now Colchester and began a conquest of the land.

Soon Roman armies had advanced as far north as the river Don and the silence of prehistory is broken as, for the first time, individual people in our region are mentioned by Roman historians.

Immediately we are in the middle of a story. It concerns that dominating northern tribe, the Brigantes. Its reigning queen, Cartimandua and her consort, Venutius, are not getting on too well – keep an eye on the handsome armour-bearer! It seems she has decided that these new invaders are powerful enough to make good allies and has agreed a peace treaty with them (whether, as the Romans said, she has also agreed to give them sovereignty over her tribe will never be known – there are no Brigantian historians).

One day, to ingratiate herself still further with the Romans, Cartimandua sends back to them, in chains, Caractacus, a rebellious British prince of the Catuvellauni tribe who had come to her court seeking asylum.

Venutius has been unhappy for some time about the cosy deal with the Romans, but treating a suppliant and guest in this way is going too far. The relationship with his wife completely breaks down. She abruptly divorces Venutius and installs the armour-bearer in his place. He raises an army and attacks: *she* calls on her new allies for help. The Romans are delighted: now they have a perfect excuse to send troops north of the Don.

The leader responsible for the pacification of what was later to became Yorkshire is Quintus Petilius Cerialis, the Roman governor of Britain who, ten years before Cartimandua asked for help, had helped to defeat Queen Boudicca. He now leads the Ninth Legion from its base at Lincoln, crosses the Humber, probably at Petuaria (Brough) and, at about two days further march north, establishes a fort on a well-positioned site between two rivers. It is given the name Eboracum (now York). Cartimandua is restored to power, but it is only a matter of time before further revolts lead to more extensive occupation and eventually to the total conquest of Brigantia; York, in time, becomes the capitol of Northern Britain. Cartumandua's story, unlike Boudicca's, remains without an ending.

The strategic siting of York had lasting effects on the subsequent history of Yorkshire, as it became the pivotal point of the all-important northern road system when the conquest moved up country. From here, for centuries, expeditions against troublesome northern tribes were organised. York connected Ermine Street, coming up from the South, with the most important forts: Calcaria (Tadcaster), Isurium Brigantium (Aldborough), Cataractonium (Catterick) and, in time, all the marching camps and forts established in the Pennines right up to Hadrian's Wall. Roads from York also went east, to Bridlington on the coast, and to Delgovicia (probably Malton).

Eboracum itself became one of the biggest military centres in Europe. Its impressive fort walls stretched along the river Ouse, strengthened with multi-angular towers, one of which can still be seen. Behind this, where the Minster now stands, was the pillar-lined main administration building. (One of its pillars, erected upside down, stands outside the South door of the Minster.) Stonegate and Petergate are on the line of the original fort's thoroughfares.

York's military importance meant that no less than two Roman emperors were in Eboracum when they died. The first was Septimius Severus in 211. His sons, Caracalla and Geta, were declared co-emperors (Caracalla murdered Geta not long afterwards). The second was Constantius Chlorus whose son, Constantine, was hailed emperor by the army in 306. He went on to Christianise the empire and move its centre from Rome to Constantinople.

Although never really officially approved, it was common for a civilian town or vicus to grow up next to a Roman fort. The one at York was located on the west side of the Ouse, where the cemetery and, probably, the yet-to-be-discovered amphitheatre were also situated. (The beheaded skeletons of possible gladiators were discovered nearby in 2004.)

Eboracum's vicus was declared to be a 'colonia' by the emperor Caracalla. This term was used for a settlement of veterans and once carried with it certain benefits including freedom from taxes, but we don't know if that was the case with York.

Isurium Brigantium (Aldborough near Boroughbridge), although only a small village today, was the second largest military settlement in the area. The road that runs next to it (mostly on the line of the A1) connected Eboracum with forts right up to the Antonine Wall, while another road branched off from it to Luguvalium (Carlisle). Aldborough's church stands on what was the forum of the town. Its amphitheatre, the largest in northern England but lost for centuries, was located in 2011 at nearby Studforth Hill, thanks to the help of geomagnetic scanners, but it has yet to be excavated. The fort itself is in the care of English Heritage.

But what of that other Yorkshire tribe, the cart-driving Parisi? It seems that they were friendly with the Romans from the beginning and so their immediate fate was rather different to that of the Brigantes. It is likely that their territory provided safe passage for Roman troops during the first phases of the conquest of the Brigantes (who were tribal rivals). If so, the Romans were suitably grateful, for there is no evidence of any violence in the capitol, Petuaria (Brough) and the area seems to have gone its own way and prospered quietly as the Parisi too came under Roman rule.

Life for ordinary farming people in Roman Yorkshire was far less influenced by the occupation than further south, where large slave-run farms provided huge amounts of grain for the army. Field systems remained much the same as before and the traditional round houses, some of them hundreds of years old, remained in use. A few villas were built, notably those at Rudston and Langton, but there is curiously little evidence that typical Roman goods like glass, kitchen ware and amphorae of wine found their way down to ordinary people. Even the mosaic floors that

survive are merely crude country versions of the more splendid ones in southern villas.

There was a fort at Hayton, a day's march from Eboracum at the foot of the Wolds, and extensive excavation nearby has revealed the remains of bath houses, a timber-lined well and stone-built buildings, as well as a number of more traditional round houses. A little further down the road at Shiptonthorpe there was another ribbon development, of wooden houses this time, probably belonging to retired soldiers. Roman export items were found in all the places associated with the fort, whereas nearby Holme-upon-Spalding-Moor, where there were industries such as potteries, had almost nothing in the way of luxury goods.

The main point of conquest (apart from providing career opportunities for aspiring young Roman commanders) was to obtain resources and taxes. In Yorkshire there was lead, coal and ironstone to be exploited and good clay to be turned into saleable pots. There were potteries at Crambeck, Knapton and Norton as well as Holme-upon-Spalding-Moor, leather tanneries at Catterick, and iron foundries in many places. Ordinary folk, no doubt, bought some of these products but they were mostly sold to the military, along with food supplies, bringing modest prosperity to the region. The security provided by the army maintained peace during years that in much of Europe were very turbulent.

This peace deteriorated during the fifth century when Anglo-Saxon raiders from Germany began to attack the coast. For many years they were successfully turned back by the army, which built defensive coastal forts at Scarborough, Filey, Flamborough, Goldsborough, Huntcliff and Ravenscar. However, Rome itself was in trouble, coming under increasing attack from the Goths, and riven with internal dissentions. It began recalling its soldiers from the outskirts of the empire. In 410 the last of the Roman army left Britain. Its inhabitants, used to someone else defending them, were now left alone to face the invaders.

YORKSHIRE FOLK:
From the tombstone in York of **Corellia Optata,** 13 years old, possibly from the vicus:

'To the spirits of the departed. Ye hidden spirits, that dwell in Pluto's Acherusian realms, whom the scanty ash and the shade, the body's image, seek after life's little day, I, the pitiable father of an innocent daughter, caught by cheating hope, lament her final end. Quintus Corellius Fortis, the father, had this made.'

PLACES TO VISIT:
Wheeldale Roman Road: near Goathland
Aldborough Roman Site: Boroughbridge, North Yorkshire
The Yorkshire Museum: Museum Gardens, York
Cawthorne Roman Camp: near Pickering, North York Moors

6

THE ANGLO-SAXONS

THE ANGLIAN INVASIONS

About thirty or forty years after the legions left, Anglo-Saxon raids intensified and times grew more unsettled. Towns rely on currency and regular supplies of food and goods; some towns in Britain were already in decline from the middle of the fifth century as administration failed. York was abandoned, and the legionary settlements at Aldborough, Catterick, Brough, Doncaster and Malton fell into disuse as their inhabitants returned to the safer countryside and an agricultural life. Government, such as it was, now rested with British tribal leaders (the modern name 'Celts' for the native people of Britain was unknown to them: they called themselves Britons) who organised things as best they could. The old Roman administrative provinces broke down into a collection of small kingdoms ruled by leaders who, for a while, claimed to be following Roman ways, but who had, in fact, become war lords. There were two main British kingdoms in Yorkshire, Ebrauc (York) and Elmet to the south-west. (The latter's existence is still remembered in village names such as Barwick-in-Elmet.)

The knowledge of writing did not, as some have claimed, entirely disappear (see *In Search of The Dark Ages* by Michael Wood) but no records have survived and so archaeology is our only way of discovering anything about this period. Money ceased to be used and was sometimes buried in hoards while its owners waited for better times. To add to the troubles the weather appears to have become wetter during the fifth century: there was serious flooding in the Vales of Pickering and York, causing people to relocate to higher land. Plague (possibly bubonic) caused widespread devastation in the Roman Empire in the sixth century, though due to the lack of written records we do not know whether it ever reached Yorkshire.

It was the Angles rather than the Saxons who were to have the most effect on our area. They came from the Baltic region and had raided the coasts of Britain for many decades before joining with the Saxons and the Jutes to mount a more sustained invasion, probably as a result of being forced from their own homelands by increasing Danish migration. There are various conflicting estimates of numbers of invaders, but recent DNA analysis shows that Yorkshire people have a greater proportion of Anglo-Saxon DNA than the population as a whole, which suggests that they came here in substantial numbers – though the old idea that they drove out the original population has long been discredited.

Curiously enough, whatever their numbers and whatever heroic battles there may have been between them and the local warrior nobility, they don't seem to have disturbed the indigenous farming population much. Sites around the county show a surprising continuity between Roman and Anglo-Saxon periods, the main change being from the fine Roman wheel-made pottery to the coarser hand-made Anglo-Saxon sort.

The newcomers regarded the remaining Roman stone buildings with superstitious awe as the work of giants and avoided them; they preferred to live in their own

rectangular wooden houses in their own villages. Such a village of some 150 timber buildings has been excavated at West Heslerton at the edge of the Wolds. The few remaining examples of Anglian wood-carving show that they were as much masters of the art as the Romans had been of stone-carving, but because wood decays so easily their work has mostly disappeared. They were also skilled in all types of smith work, including goldsmithing, and had discovered how to make a form of steel. It was their heavier ploughs that allowed the clay lands in the Vale of York to be tilled for the first time.

ANGLIAN YORKSHIRE

By the early seventh century Angles had overcome the British rulers of Ebrauc and established the Anglian kingdom of Deira in the old Parisi territory, stretching from the Humber north to the Tees and west through the Vale of York to the borders of the British Kingdom of Elmet, which was later captured. At some point York (Eboracum, Caer Ebrauc, now called Eoforwic: Boar Town) became the capital, though there was still superstitious reluctance to reinhabit the old fortress: the Anglian town was built right on its edge, near Fishergate. Anglian territorial land-grabs soon extended north of the Tees as far as the Forth, eventually taking in the old Roman Province of Bernicia and the whole kingdom became known as Northumbria.

There is not room here to go into the complicated history of Northumbria, which contains enough murders, betrayals and family feuds to provide material for several television series. Suffice it to say that few Northumbrian rulers died in bed.

Originally the Angles were pagans, with their own gods: Tiw, Woden, Thor, Frigga, after whom some of our days of the week are named. The conquered Britons were nominally Christian, though the distance to Rome and the Pope meant that until Pope Gregory (AD 540–604) sent a mission to Britain they had been more or less forgotten by the Roman Church. One of the main pagan shrines in Deira was at Goodmanham, near Market Weighton. In 625 King Edwin of Northumbria, conqueror of Elmet, who had just survived an assassination attempt, was celebrating the pagan spring festival at his summer palace near Pocklington. His wife was a Christian princess who had her own bishop, Paulinus. He had been sent from Rome by Pope Gregory entrusted with a mission to convert the Anglo-Saxons to Christianity. The Venerable Bede, who lived about 100 years later, describes in *The Ecclesiastical History of the English People* how the king was persuaded to hold a great conference to consider whether to convert or not. Moved by the arguments, the chief priest of Woden rode to the shrine of the god and desecrated it by throwing his spear through the doorway. It was then burned. Edwin was baptised two years later and thereafter the people of Northumbria were theoretically Christian (though old ways died hard).

The problem was that Paulinus' version of Christianity wasn't the only one on offer.

During the years in which Britain had been forgotten by Rome, Irish monks, led by St Columba, had become established on the island of Iona near Mull. They had spread their teachings in northern England. Their way of worshipping, brought to Ireland many years before by St Patrick, had, over time, developed its own idiosyncrasies and traditions unknown in Rome. They determined the time of Easter differently; they allowed married clergy; they had different tonsures (ways of shaving the head) and their monasteries followed their own independent rules rather than those approved by Rome. These differences might not seem very serious to us but to the newly converted Christians it was important to feel that they were performing everything correctly so that God was not offended. The Irish Church honoured the Pope but it also honoured its own traditions. The Roman Church (i.e. the church headed by the Pope in Rome) was keen to establish its power as the arbiter of Christian belief and do away with disagreement. By 663 the conflict between the Irish and Roman ways was beginning to destabilise the royal family. The king of Northumbria at the time was no longer Edwin, but Oswiu. He favoured the Irish Church, but his wife and his son, whose favourite priest was a pushy young monk from Rome, called Wilfred, favoured the reforming Roman one.

The chief bone of contention was the date of Easter. By this time the two systems of determining it were so out of alignment that the king was celebrating Christ's Resurrection with feasting while his wife and son were still fasting for Lent. Oswiu decided to settle the matter once and for all by calling a synod (a meeting of the heads of the Church) at the newly founded abbey of Streoneshalh (now Whitby) which was ruled by the Abbess Hild, a supporter of the Irish Church. Both sides were represented, though as the representative of the Roman Church didn't know much Anglo-Saxon, Wilfred (very conveniently) spoke for him. Bishop Colman spoke for the Irish side. Many points were made by both and the debate went back and forth, but in the end the king decided that the reformers had the best arguments. He declared that from then on, all Christian worship in Northumbria would follow the practices of the Roman Church. Wilfred's career was greatly enhanced. Always contentious (he maintained a bodyguard of warriors) he went on to become Bishop of Northumbria and York, to found many monasteries and, after his death, to achieve that highest of Christian honours, sainthood.

The majority of the population may not have known or cared a lot about the date of Easter. They went on honouring holy wells and sacred trees as they always had (and, it appears, always will!) but the reformist priests celebrated their civilising victory by beginning to build lots of churches, some in stone. Most, like Wilfred's Ripon Cathedral, were too small for subsequent tastes and were rebuilt. Many were destroyed later in Viking attacks. However, the amazingly atmospheric St Wilfred's crypt at Ripon and the Anglian part of All Saints in Ledsham still give some idea of what they were like. A few large stone Anglian crosses remain, demonstrating fine carving of entwined animals and plants. There are three at Ilkley, two at Otley and several more at Dewsbury.

The real legacy of the Anglo-Saxons is in the English language. It has changed through time and picked up words from other languages, but the descendants of a huge number of its words are still in use (including most of the ones in this sentence) and it produced vivid written works such as *Beowulf* and *The Seafarer*, which are still studied and enjoyed (influencing modern writers like Tolkien).

Then, in 793, the Vikings attacked the monastery at Lindisfarne and for the Anglian Kingdom of Northumbria time began to run out.

YORKSHIRE FOLK:

Caedmon is the first poet writing in Anglo-Saxon whose name is known. He was an illiterate cowherd at Streoneshalh monastery (now Whitby Abbey) in the days of St Hild (614-680). Although unlearned in the Anglo-Saxon poetic art he was, according to the eighth-century historian Bede, given the gift of composition in a dream. Thereafter he became fully ordained and composed many inspired Christian songs not in Latin, as was the tradition, but in the Anglo-Saxon vernacular.

PLACES TO VISIT:

St Gregory's Minster: Anglo-Saxon church near Kirbymoorside, North Yorkshire

Goodmanham: Site of the Temple to Woden. You can't see it as it's probably under the church but there's a good pub...

Crypt of Ripon Cathedral: Unchanged since the seventh century

7

THE VIKINGS

The destruction of Lindisfarne was the first of regular Viking raids that eventually turned into invasion. The word 'Viking' really means 'raider'. A Viking was a man (though there is some evidence that there were women as well) who left his own homeland to gain fame and fortune in someone else's. During this period, increasing population growth in Scandinavia meant that acquiring land – the only way to become an important person – was becoming more and more difficult. The swiftest way for young men to make a name for themselves was to join together and take their chances across the seas in raiding ventures. Vikings came from Norway as well as Denmark. They were quite capable of raiding each other.

Tales of the incredible wealth and gold of English monasteries had spread to Scandinavia, but, like the Anglo-Saxons before them, men wanted land as well as the rich plunder, preferably land with captured slaves to work it. There were many other raids along the Northumbrian coast in the years following 793, but in 865 a more serious threat arose. A 'Great Heathen Army' of Danes sailed from the Low Countries to East Anglia. They were led by the splendidly named Ivarr the Boneless and his brothers

Halfdan and Ubba, already war-hardened veterans of campaigns in Europe. In the following year they sailed up the Humber and headed towards York.

The Kingdom of Northumbria was, as usual, occupied with fighting between rival claimants for the throne. The rivals in this instance were Aelle and Osberht. Taken by surprise by the huge army of invaders, they forgot their grievances and joined forces, but too late: both were killed in the subsequent fighting. Ivarr is supposed to have had the Blood Eagle cut on Aelle (a ritualised method of execution) in revenge for his having killed Ivarr's father, Ragnar Hairybreeches, in a pit of snakes, but this is, let us hope, probably just legend.

In 876 Halfdan shared out Northumbria between his followers and, as the Anglo-Saxon Chronicle records, 'they proceeded to plough and support themselves'. Bernicia, the northern half of Northumbria, doesn't seem to have interested the Vikings as much as the richer southern half, Deira. With its capital at Yorvik (the latest version of York's name) Deira became the Danish Kingdom of York and, ultimately, Yorkshire.

It was not, of course, the only part of Britain conquered by the Danes. King Alfred of Wessex halted their southern progress at the Battle of Edington in 878 and forced the leader of the southern Danish army to sign a treaty that established the limit of Danish conquests. They were to keep York, Nottingham, Derby, Lincoln and all the eastern counties above London. In those places the law of the Danes, rather than that of the Anglo-Saxons, was to run and so the area became known as the Danelaw. The Danes in England remained the biggest threat to Anglo-Saxon kings, siding with their enemies at home and in Scandinavia, inviting invasion from outside. One king, Aethelred, even tried genocide to get rid of them (though not in Yorkshire), but in vain.

In the early years of the invasion those sources of literacy, monasteries, were widely destroyed. As their surviving monks were occupied with more urgent things than writing accounts about the invaders, once again we do not have a lot of information about the number of new settlers.

People didn't distinguish between raiders from Denmark and raiders from Norway or elsewhere; they were all just Danes. Many Yorkshire villages have the Danish suffixes –by or –thorpe, and about a third of place names in the East and North Ridings in Domesday Book are of Scandinavian origin, which suggests that local people must, at the very least, have been widely influenced by Scandinavian languages. Many words in our language are Scandinavian in origin, Norse (Norwegian) as well as Danish. (West Yorkshire in particular, was influenced by Norwegians from the Viking kingdom of Dublin who began to farm land in and around the Pennines that hadn't previously been used.) Yorkshire people still use 'beck' instead of 'stream' and 'bairns' for children. York streets are called 'gates' just as they are in Norway and there are a number of Scandinavian words in Yorkshire dialect for types of land: 'carr' (marsh); 'slack' (valley); 'gill' (ravine); and 'holm' (island).

Once they had established their kingdom, the Danish rulers of our area divided Yorkshire and its neighbouring Linsey in to three administrative parts called 'thridings' (thirdings) from which we get the Yorkshire Ridings. These were further divided into wapentakes (from the showing of weapons at assemblies). The invaders then converted to Christianity (possibly to impress the locals) and settled down to trade, Vikings no longer.

Little remains above ground to show they were here. None of their churches survive, though many were built by people keen to acquire status in their new kingdom, but a number of carved Viking stones and 'hogback' tombs can still be found. A few crosses remain, such as the famous Nunburnholme Cross, which include pagan as well as Christian imagery.

Our knowledge of Viking life has been enormously enhanced by the extensive York excavations of 1976–81. The oxygen-free environment of the site at Coppergate led to the preservation of a huge range of materials such as leather, cloth and wood, as well as timber buildings and the debris of domestic and manufacturing life. The Jorvik Viking Centre was opened to the public in 1984 and is the most important museum of Viking life in the country. It reveals a way of life that strongly contrasts with the image of the bloodthirsty pillager. Jorvik, it seems, was a busy manufacturing and trading centre, with a flourishing river trade up and down the Ouse, importing high-quality goods such as pottery and silk from all over Europe. Its well-nourished citizens (only about 8cm shorter than us) were clean and well-dressed – Danes were famously natty dressers, with a taste for bright colours – possessing a wide range of combs, ear-scoops, tweezers, nail cleaners and toothpicks. The men did not – repeat, did not – ever wear horned helmets but they did appreciate a good sword as a sign of wealth and status. The women favoured the strange objects called tortoise brooches which were worn in pairs on the breast with a string of beads between. It was during the Viking period that the present layout of York streets was created.

Control of York and the rest of Northumbria passed through many different hands over time, including those of the Norwegian Vikings from Dublin, but its last king, Eric Bloodaxe, was killed in 954 and it was then incorporated into what was fast becoming the Kingdom of England. Jorvik continued to flourish, however, and life went on much the same for the people of our county for 100 years.

But bad times were coming ...

YORKSHIRE FOLK:

Guthfrith: According to Symeon of Durham's *History of the Church of* Durham Guthfrith, a Christian Viking was appointed King of York in 878 after St Cuthbert appeared in a dream to Abbot Eadred of Carlisle, telling him to find a lad named Guthfrith. This boy, said the Saint, had been sold to a widow. The Abbot must find him and pay the widow the price of his freedom and then present him to the army, telling them that it was the Saint's wish he be made king. 'Let the bracelet [of kingship] be placed on his right arm!' said the Saint.

Eadred did as he was commanded but Guthfrith ruled only for a few years before dying and being buried in York Minster.

PLACES TO VISIT:

The Jorvik Centre: York
The Nunburnholme Cross: in St James' Church at Nunburnholme near Pocklington
Collection of **Viking age carved stones:** St Wilfred's Church, Burnsall. The church is on east side of the B6160 at the north end of Burnsall village

8

THE NORMANS

YORKSHIRE BEFORE THE NORMAN CONQUEST

By the eleventh century Yorkshire, still part of Northumbria, had been farmed for hundreds if not thousands of years. Farming people worked hard to get the best out of the available land with whatever methods they had available but they weren't living in some sort of rural idyll. Most land didn't produce much more than a bare subsistence for most of the year. A bad harvest caused by poor weather or disease in stock or crops meant famine and the deaths of the weakest in the community: the young, the old, and animals. Evidence from tooth enamel, even during the Roman period, shows that many people experienced famine in their childhood (when the enamel is laid down). Taxes and sporadic periods of fighting, with armies or raiders living off the land, added to these problems, so it is easy to see that ordinary people were often desperate to find a reliable source of help in bad times. In the most extreme need people sold themselves or their children as thralls (slaves) – thralls got fed while free folk starved.

It is often forgotten in our horror at the cruelty inflicted on nineteenth-century black slaves that slavery of one sort or another was an essential motor of most economies for most of human history. It was the main way, apart from using animals, of providing cheap energy. (As we know from recent prosecutions, slavery may have gone underground in our own day but it still exists.) The Viking raids were as much about slaves as they were about gold. The Dublin Vikings, for example, supplied Irish slaves to the big slave markets of Byzantium and the Middle East. Some of their manacles can be seen in the National Museum of Ireland in Dublin. How many thralls there were in Yorkshire at this time we don't know because, being the lowest of the low, they were seldom recorded, except when a fine had to be paid to their owners after a slave had been injured or killed.

If you preferred to avoid the shame of slavery and keep your free status one way in which you could get additional support in hard times was by offering to work for richer people. You would still have to keep on farming your own land as well, but your employer then had some obligations towards helping you. Inevitably those who offered their work to a more powerful person in this way quickly became tied to that service; thus, long before the Conquest there were people in our county who, while having the title of freemen, were serfs in all but name.

The actual methods of farming varied with different types of land. Holderness, for example, with its rich alluvial soil had extensive cornfields. The Wolds were now more lightly farmed, with large numbers of grazing animals. The boggy undrained carr lands around the Ouse and Humber were still wooded and unfarmed, while further west on the lighter sandstones wood pasture (open woodland with grazing among the trees) was more usual. In the Pennines oats and rye were grown in small fields.

Over the years the vast estates stolen from the monasteries and redistributed to Viking followers were divided up between the children and dependants of the original owners. This produced smaller landholdings whose lords lived locally and could keep an eye on the people who farmed on the estate. Villages of any sort were fairly rare in Anglian and Scandinavian Yorkshire, most people living in scattered farmsteads or small groups of houses. However, towards the end of the period there is some evidence that in places like the Vale of Pickering whole villages were being planned. If you are a subsistence farmer, getting together with others is a much more efficient way of farming. Land, tools and work can be shared, and livestock herded together and better protected. In a planned village each house had its own croft (a strip of land behind) for growing vegetables or raising hens and pigs, while two big communally owned fields provided arable and grazing. This was the beginning of the open field system which was to be further developed in the Middle Ages. Whether these planned villages were the result of communal planning or imposed by the local landowner to maximise tax-gathering potential is unclear.

People could still take over hitherto unfarmed land or clear woodland to add to their holdings and hunt or forage for wild food as their ancestors had done. Kings handed down laws, but it was hard to enforce them and most justice depended heavily on whatever was the custom locally.

THE NORMAN CONQUEST

In 954 Eric Bloodaxe, the last king of York, was killed at the Battle of Stainmore and the kingdom was annexed to Wessex to become part of the kingdom of England. A local earl was put in charge of what was now called the Earldom of Northumbria. Its Scandinavian sympathies remained as strong as ever and Jorvik's trade and prosperity continued.

Some of the locals must have been pleased when, between 1016 and 1042, England was ruled by the famous King Canute and became part of his Scandinavian empire. By this time the relationships between Danish and Anglo-Saxon nobility had become deeply intertwined; into the mix now came the Normans in the person of Emma, Canute's wife. She was the great-granddaughter of a Viking warlord called Rollo, who had been bribed with Normandy ('Northman's land') by the French king to stop his raiding. Her previous husband, the English king Aethelred, known to history as Aethelred the Unready, but actually nicknamed Unferth, which just meant that he never took advice. He had been killed in battle with Canute, but Emma didn't appear to object to marrying his conqueror and it seems to have been a happy marriage. Emma's sons by Aethelred, Edward and Alfred, were brought up in Normandy by her relations.

After Canute's death his own sons inherited his lands but they died young and his empire fell to pieces. Edward was brought back from Normandy with an entourage of Norman friends to rule England, a country he didn't really know. Inevitably he made mistakes, the worst of which was appointing a southerner called Tosdig to be Earl of Northumbria. Tosdig and his brother Harold were the sons of a powerful Anglo-Saxon lord called Godwin. It didn't take long before his high-handed ways offended the stiff-necked northerners he had been sent to rule. They rose in revolt and threw his men out of York, inviting a more friendly noble to take his place.

By this time his brother Harold had become King Edward's closest advisor and so the king sent him to make peace. As it quickly became clear that Tosdig had gone too far ever to be accepted back as Earl, Harold agreed that he should be exiled. From that moment the two brothers were enemies and Tosdig worked not just to get back his earldom, but to undermine the kingdom. Eventually he persuaded Harald (note the difference in spelling) Hardrada (king of Norway) to raise an army and invade England, claiming the throne through his descent from Canute.

In 1066 Edward (now known as the Confessor for his pious ways) fell ill. Facing threats from both Norway and Normandy he chose Harold Godwinson, an experienced warrior, as his successor rather than a closer but much younger relative. The crown did not automatically pass to the eldest son in those days, as it was to do under the Normans: the king could name his own successor as long as the Witangemot (the King's Council) agreed. This was an advantage in a violent world of warfare where kings were liable to die early, leaving young children. It was a disadvantage if, as in this case, the throne had already been offered to someone else. Duke William the Bastard (as he called himself) was the only son of the unmarried Duke Robert of Normandy. He swore that Edward had promised *him* the throne some years before. While impossible to verify after such a long time, this is quite possibly true – though kings have a right to change their minds and clearly Edward had done so. One thing was certain: William, who had spent his entire life fighting for land, was not going to let the opportunity to win himself a kingdom pass him by.

In the summer of 1066 Tosdig and Harald Hardrada arrived in England with about 8,000 men. They sailed up the Ouse, as their forefathers had done, and defeated an English army at Fulford, near York. Having received the surrender of York and taken local hostages they offered peace to Northumbria in return for support for Hardrada's claim to the English throne. They also commanded that additional important hostages be brought to their camp at Stamford Bridge on the Derwent. There they settled down to wait for their arrival in the unseasonably hot September weather.

Meanwhile Harold Godwinson was in the south, mustering men to deal with the threat of William of Normandy's invasion. The news of the return of his brother Tosdig with a Norwegian army must have come as a horrible blow, but Edward had not mistaken his ability as a warrior. He marched his army 200 miles north in four days and took Hardrada's men (some of whom had removed their chainmail because of the heat) completely by surprise.

According to the not-always-reliable Anglo-Saxon Chronicle, one huge Norse axeman held up Harold's army by defending the bridge all alone, like the Roman Horatius, until stabbed from below by a Saxon, who floated under the bridge on a half-barrel. His heroism didn't save the Norwegians, nor did the arrival of reinforcements. Hardrada's army was completely routed and he and Tosdig were killed.

Harold Godwinson had no time to celebrate his victory, for almost immediately news reached him that Duke William had landed. He and his battle-wearied men then marched south to their defeat at Hastings.

No doubt the people of York and the surrounding areas were glad that the fighting had moved off south. Maybe some of the more politically minded discussed the possibility of calling on the Danes or the Scots to help them if this Norman Duke managed by some fluke to defeat Harold. They certainly didn't foresee the disaster that lay ahead.

WILLIAM TAKES CONTROL

How did William, with only 7,000 men, manage to conquer the country? It was partly because many Anglo-Saxons seem to have had a fatalistic expectation of defeat and partly because their old way of fighting on foot with axes, inherited from Germanic forebears, was no match for William's heavy cavalry. Southern England was swiftly subdued, but in the old Viking heartland of Jorvik things were different.

Only two years after the Battle of Hastings, in 1068, William's newly imposed taxes caused the first of the northern revolts against him, but the rebels failed to gain enough support and fled. In response William deployed the latest weapon in his armoury: a castle.

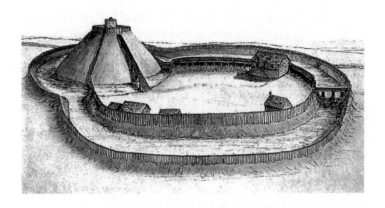

Normans had been building castles in France for some time, but they were very unusual in Britain. Forget impressive piles of stone: these were either quickly built raised rings topped with wooden palisades, or the artificial flat-topped hills called mottes on which wooden towers, known as keeps, were built. Good examples of mottes can be seen in South Yorkshire at Bradfield, Mexborough and Thorne. An area next to the motte, known as the bailey, also surrounded by a ditch and palisade, might be added, providing room for horses, stores, etc. At Skipsea, built soon after the Conquest, the impressive motte was connected to the bailey by a causeway across what was once a tidal mere.

The function of these small castles was to provide troops with a better vantage point and a greater degree of protection from attack. They were also a blatant statement of dominance and were bitterly resented by the locals who were forced to labour building them. A castle of this sort could be raised in a week and William commanded one to be built in York, probably where Clifford's Tower is now. He also diverted the River Foss to fill a moat around it, which caused large-scale flooding. The flooded area became known as the King's Fishpond which is why, though the water has long since gone, the area still retains the name 'Foss Islands'.

William Malet and 500 men were left to garrison the new castle, but the following year William's new earl in Durham was burnt to death in his house and his men slaughtered in another uprising. The rebels moved on York, but the new castle held out and was relieved just in time by William, who now built a *second* castle, the Old Baile, on the other side of the river Ouse.

If William's intention was to deter rebels from sailing up the river it was thwarted in September 1069 by a third uprising. This was the most serious, and William came very close to losing his new country. The northern rebels had offered the crown of England to King Sweyn of Denmark and he landed with a huge army of Danes, sailing up the Ouse in the traditional Viking manner. The Norman garrisons of the two castles ill-advisedly sallied out and were cut down. The conquest hung by a thread. Then William seized the offensive by offering Sweyn and his men more gold than they could resist or the rebels afford to match. The Danes sailed home rich and content, leaving the north to face the Conqueror's revenge.

THE HARRYING OF THE NORTH

Now began a systematic campaign of terror intended to break all resistance to the new masters. How extensive it was is a matter of debate among historians, but our knowledge of similar modern campaigns in places like Syria points to there having been considerable brutality. The Anglo-Saxon Chronicle records that William 'laid waste all the shire'. At least part of York seems to have been burnt, including the Minster, but that was just the start; his army marched through the countryside around York and Durham, killing everyone they could find including the animals. They burnt the villages and hamlets, the ploughs and tools, the grain and stores of all kinds, depriving not only the rebels but most of the local population of food.

How many people died in the subsequent famine we don't know (though the figure of 100,000 given by a later writer is probably an exaggeration). No doubt many hid – they certainly hid their money, as a number of hoards of silver dating to this period have been found around York, and the fact that they were never reclaimed is significant. Yorkshire has been through many bad times but this must surely have been one of the worst. In Domesday Book, compiled seventeen years later, 480 Yorkshire vills (or townships) are designated wholly 'waste'. This didn't necessarily mean that no one lived there, but it does suggest a very high level of poverty from which it took years to recover.

After the Harrying, William resumed his castle building. The Anglo-Saxon Chronicle gloomily records 'castles he caused to be made and poor men to be greatly oppressed'. In time the combustible wooden towers and palisades of the most important castles were replaced with stone keeps and solid defensive walls by their Norman owners. The less important were abandoned, the locals, presumably, having been sufficiently subdued.

William rewarded many of his followers generously with lands in the south taken from their Anglo-Saxon owners. However, in the troublesome north only a few men could be trusted to be strong and ruthless enough to hold onto the territory. These men ruled vast estates with iron fists and built their own castles with which to do so. William de Warrenne got lands in South Yorkshire and built Conisbrough Castle; Ilbert de Laci got the Honour of Pontifract and a huge part of West Yorkshire; William de Perci (whose family name is remembered in Bolton and Kilnwick Percy) got Topcliffe, near Thirsk; Mauger le Vavasour built Hazelwood Castle on his lands near York. The whole of Holderness went first to a Flemish soldier called Drogo de la Beuvrière who built Skipsea Castle, and then to the unpleasantly corrupt Bishop Odo. A relative of William, Alain Rufus (Alan the Red), reputedly one of the richest men in Europe, received a large slice of North Yorkshire and built castles at Richmond (named after his estate in France, Richemont, meaning the strong hill), Knaresborough and Middleham. Other important Norman castles were built at Scarborough, Pickering and Helmsley.

A castle can be held against a king as well as for him and in the turbulent years following the death of the Conqueror the new great men began to use them to make themselves greater still. In 1135 a civil war broke out between the supporters of Matilda, granddaughter of the Conqueror and heir to the throne, and those of her cousin Stephen, whose claim was that he was the nearest *male* (and therefore better) heir to the throne.

During the nineteen years of the war 'every man built him castles and held them against the king ... and filled them with devils ... men said that God and his angels slept'.

The whole of England was drawn into conflict and in the north the Scots took advantage of the strife to invade Yorkshire.

YORKSHIRE AND THE SCOTS

The Romans had never conquered the Pictish tribes north of the Antonine Wall and by the eleventh century raiding back and forth across the Solway Firth, the ancient border between the Picto-Gallic Kingdom of Alba and the Anglian kingdom of Northumbria, had long been endemic. Loyalties changed swiftly; sometimes Northumbrian lords might ally themselves with the Scots to attack their enemies; at others they might find themselves raided by their past allies, or lead war parties deep into Scottish territory themselves. Earl Siward (nicknamed The Stout) whose burial mound is near the Universityof York, had managed, with a heavy hand, the tricky job of keeping peace in the north during the early part of the eleventh century – he once defeated

Macbeth – but after his death Scottish raids increased and continued sporadically for centuries.

Scotland became a united kingdom in 1018 and subsequent Scottish kings, with their eyes on expanding their territory, began to make more serious incursions into northern England, sometimes seizing land in Northumbria (of which Yorkshire was then still a part). What northern folk cared most about for hundreds of years, therefore, was not who became king of England but what was he going to do about the Scots? Yorkshire people faced north, not south.

In 1071 William the Conqueror invaded Scotland (for reasons too complicated to explain here), and defeated its king, Malcolm. He forced Malcolm to acknowledge himself as overlord. In subsequent years parents of several heirs to the Scottish throne, impressed by this Norman military success, sent them to be educated in England to get the Norman touch. Once William was dead, however, these same heirs did not feel that they owned any loyalty to the English crown (on which one or two had a reasonable claim).

In 1136, the Scottish king David intervened in the before-mentioned civil war between Stephen and Matilda and invaded Northumbria several times. His ostensible intention was to support William's granddaughter, Matilda, but in reality he wanted to extend his landholdings. His most serious invasion seems to have been pretty violent even by the standards of that violent civil war; he crossed the Tees with a sizeable army and raided Craven.

In York the great lords gathered to consider their options. As usual, none of them really trusted any of the others, but Archbishop Thurstan of York did his best to unite them. They marched out to meet David's army north of Northallerton, taking with them a cart on which were raised the consecrated banners of the minsters of York, Beverley and Ripon, hence the following battle is known as the Battle of the Standards. Despite the size of the Scottish army it was routed with considerable losses. David escaped to Carlisle, but the English lords did not follow up their victory. They went instead for a settlement which left them free to continue their civil war without Scottish interference. All the northern part of Northumbria (excluding Newcastle and Bamborough) down as far as the Tees, was given to David's son, who became its earl.

Scotland did not begin at the Tees for long, however. About thirty years later Matilda's able son Henry II drove out the Scots and regained most of the land they had taken.

After this time Yorkshire and Northumberland were more or less considered as separate counties and each went its own way.

MONASTERIES

The old Anglian monasteries had been so plundered by the Vikings that none remained north of the Trent by the time of the Conquest. After the Conquest William and subsequent Norman kings deliberately re-established the old religious foundations and created new ones to strengthen their hold on a people whose reliance on religion may now seem unfamiliar to us. These new northern monasteries went on, in the next couple of centuries, to become among the most successful and rich in England.

William himself founded Selby Abbey and other foundations soon followed: St Mary's in York, Lastingham, Whitby, Kirkham Priory, Rievaulx, Fountains, Jervaulx, Byland, Kirkstall and many more.

The subject of monasteries is an interesting one but it is too large to go into any great detail here. There were many orders (or types) of monks and nuns, all of which were based in some way on the earliest, the Benedictine Order, founded by St Benedict in AD 529. Each subsequent Order, whether Augustinian, Carthusian, Carmelite, Cistercian or one of their offshoots, was founded in response to what was seen as the degeneration of the original idea; they were attempts, in a world that insisted on changing, to get back to Benedict's original purity and simplicity.

There was, however, a basic conflict between the desire to separate oneself from the world to focus on a simple life of prayer, and Christ's insistence that his followers help the poor and those who suffer. The latter required resources, which demanded attention to the worldly concerns of income and production. Monasteries tried over many centuries to reconcile both. Their success varied, but for the poorest in their communities they were, on the whole, a source not just of spiritual but real material support.

All monasteries had to be self-sufficient. A generous founder might gift enough land to make this easy: a mean one might just give the least useful land on his estate (or her estate – nunneries were sometimes founded or supported by rich women). Either way, it was up to the monks, initially, to make the best of what they were given. Some monasteries were spectacularly successful, becoming not just self-sufficient, but major producers of goods, going into business, acquiring more land and employing lay brothers (a sort of monkish servant thought to be unsuited to higher things) to do the hard labour. Rievaulx, for example, which began its life as a remote place for Cistercian monks following a strict regime of work and prayer, eventually accumulated 6,000 acres, produced lead and iron and supported huge flocks of sheep whose wool was sold to buyers from all over Europe. By the time it was dissolved, under Henry VIII, it even owned a prototype blast furnace.

Jervaulx Abbey in Wensleydale rose from being an almost starving colony of monks from Byland to breeding horses and inventing Wensleydale cheese.

The richest monastery in the north was St Mary's Abbey in York. Founded in the 1083 by Alan the Red (he of Richmond Castle), it acquired estates all over the county and employed large numbers of York citizens as craftspeople, servants, laundresses and so on. It was free from all sorts of

obligations to the king and owned 'the Liberty of Bootham' just outside the city walls. The 'Liberty' was a successful trading area that enjoyed the privileges of the abbey.

Sad to relate, the holy calling of monks did not exempt them from conflict. In York, where the citizens resented monkish privilege, there were occasional fights between town and cassock in which people were killed. In other areas the conflicts were often over rents owed to the monastery or infringement of commoners' rights or even over monks poaching.

Less violent problems arose occasionally between monasteries and groups of their own monks who believed that the rules were becoming too lax and their brothers degenerate. With permission from their abbots (who were probably glad to get rid of them) small groups might go off to found stricter houses elsewhere.

Unfortunately, the simple life is not simple to maintain, and some of the monasteries founded by these groups would go on to become rich and successful in their turn. The immensely successful Fountains Abbey was founded in this way by disillusioned monks from St Mary's.

Yorkshire was noted for its many small nunneries. Examples include St Clement's, York, Handall near Whitby, Kirklees, Swine, Watton and Marrick. They are remembered in the names of Nun Appleton, Nunthorpe and Nunburnholme, near Pocklington. Most were ill-endowed and poor, with, it is estimated, only half the income of the monasteries. Unresponsive bishops received complaints year after year from them about poor food, and lack of clothes and bedclothes. Unresponsive abbesses received reciprocal complaints from the bishops about the nuns' ever-mounting debts. The situation was made worse by Scottish raids, which left some nunneries in a semi-ruinous state and dispersed their inhabitants.

Why so many Yorkshire women sought refuge in them may reflect on the poverty of the county rather than the character of Yorkshire men, although a bride of Christ was usually required to have a dowry paid for her to the nunnery (though the practice was strictly forbidden by canon law).

As long as pious lay people went on giving monasteries land and money, it was hard to focus on spiritual matters, but easy to provide food for the poor, alms for the disabled and hospitals for the sick and aged. One of the largest hospitals was St Leonard's in York, founded, it is said, by King Athelstan. It had beds for over 200 people, as well as, later in the Middle Ages, a 'bairn house' for foundlings (with its own milch cow). Before the Reformation there were some ninety hospitals in Yorkshire, run by monks and nuns. Afterwards there were none.

Monasteries and nunneries were an important part of the life of the community from the Conquest until they were closed by Henry VIII. The effects of their closure on Yorkshire people will be considered later.

NORMAN TOWNS

Secular lords were just as keen as abbots to increase their revenues. One way of doing this was to establish boroughs (towns) alongside their castles, or at some suitable place such as a road junction or river landing. Weekly markets could be held there, encouraging trading; that trade (and the right to do it) could then be taxed by the local lord. A yearly fair was even more lucrative, bringing in folk and goods from further afield. Charters could be obtained – at a price – from the king for both market and fair. Many of Yorkshire's old market towns and cities were founded in this way by Norman lords.

The market place was the main feature of the new boroughs, with plots of land, called burgages, surrounding it, often in a grid pattern. You can still see evidence of these grids in the ground plan of places like Pickering and Richmond. The owner of such a plot was a freeman (probably not a woman, unless she was a widow who had inherited it from her husband – Norman, unlike Anglo-Saxon law, discouraged women's ownership of land). He was known as a burgess and usually had various rights and duties associated with his town. His burgage plot was usually long and thin with room for a house or cottage and an area called the toft for growing vegetables or keeping pigs or hens. Such plots can be seen in many Yorkshire villages.

Some of the new boroughs did not thrive – Skipsea borough is an example – but others did, and by the thirteenth century Yorkshire had well over forty successful towns, far more than before the Conquest. Three of the earliest and most successful were created next to the castles of Richmond, Pontefract and Tickhill. Doncaster was founded where the Fossard family had erected a castle on the site of the old Roman fort guarding the Don crossing. At Sheffield William de Louvetot established a successful market that stretched uphill from his castle, built a mill (another useful source of revenue), a bridge and a hospital.

At Scarborough the borough grew up around the church of St Mary, under the shadow of the castle and near to the harbour. Helmsley, Pickering and Skipton boroughs were all founded next to their castles, as was Knaresborough. Roger de Mowbray, after whom the Vale is named, founded Thirsk, one of the most successful market towns in the north. It had *two* annual fairs, at the Feasts of St Luke and St James, as well as a weekly market.

It was not only secular lords who founded boroughs on their land. The Archbishop of York, who owned vast estates, sponsored the borough of Ripon, where the burgage plots surrounding the large market place remain pretty well unchanged. The boughs of Beverley, Otley and Patrington were also sponsored by him. His fellow Bishop of Durham sponsored boroughs at Hedon and Northallerton.

Abbots and priors got in on the act as well, founding new towns just outside the walls of their abbeys and priories. Selby, an inland port, was completely transformed when the Benedictine abbey was built. At Whitby (Hild's old Streoneshalh) the abbot of the re-founded abbey high on the cliffs established a borough below it on either side of the river Esk. At a place they called Wyke, the monks of Meaux Abbey diverted the last few hundred yards of the river Hull into a straight channel and laid out the grid of a new town. Later known as Kingston-on-Hull, this was to become the most successful of the new boroughs. Its situation made it perfect as a place to trade goods from Holderness and the Wolds, and as a supply station for traders going up the Ouse. Wyke flourished and by the end of the thirteenth century only London and Boston in lincolnshire carried more trade.

Other boroughs successful and unsuccessful were also founded by navigable rivers or the sea. In the years before his friendship with King David led to his being given lands in Scotland, Robert de Brus (an ancestor of the more famous Robert), founded an important fishing borough at Yarm in Teeside. Bridlington, though an ancient town by Norman times, did not really flourish until Walter de Gant built a priory there, leading to subsequent kings licensing both the port and an annual fair (it eventually had three!).

Parts of York may have been destroyed during the Harrying of the North, but it was soon rebuilt and became once more the most important city in the county, the only one at the time to have city walls instead of just boundary ditches. The new minster was started by Thomas of Bayeux, who was made archbishop in 1070; you can still see the crypt of this church below the present minster. Norman kings relied heavily on the loyalty of the Archbishop of York and the Bishop of Durham to assist with the administration and control of the north. They greased that loyalty with gifts to them and to their cathedral chapters, which became very rich.

These gifts were mostly of land or precious items, not actual silver coins, which were still not in widespread use. Kings had real war chests with real silver in them to pay soldiers but they were always short of actual cash. Finance was in its infancy and borrowing money difficult, so when William the Conqueror needed money to pay for the invasion of England he turned to the Jewish money lenders established in Europe. Forbidden by their own religious laws to charge interest to other Jews, they were quite happy to lend to people outside their faith, for a price. William immediately grasped that the availability of credit freed him to do more. He invited several Jews to come to England, under his protection, and gave them licences to travel throughout the kingdom – something that was usually not allowed. Laws were even made to ensure that their debtors repaid them. Many came to York and settled in Coney Street and, as people always need to borrow money, they prospered.

Unfortunately for York's Jews, the launch of the Crusades stirred up the sort of religious extremism that we are still paying for today. In the Middle Ages ignorance and intolerance of others' beliefs was universal; all non-Christians were at risk in Europe – especially if they were rich. Just like today, people were easily inflamed by some imagined atrocity.

On the night of 16 March 1190, as the new King Richard I was about to set off on Crusade, a mob of York citizens, egged on by three local landowners who owed huge sums to the York Jews, began rioting and plundering Jewish houses. The Jews, believing that they were under the king's protection, took refuge in York Castle, where Clifford's Tower now stands, but the landowners brought up siege engines to storm it. Eventually, seeing that the wooden castle would soon have to surrender, the Jews set fire to it and cut the throats of their wives and children, asking their rabbi to do the same to them. At dawn the few surviving Jews, having been promised mercy in return for Christian baptism, walked from the burnt-out keep and were promptly cut down. One hundred and eighty Jews died that night.

The king was furious, mostly at the insult to himself as their protector. He forced the landowners to pay their debts – into his own coffers. No one was ever punished in any other way. Jews returned to York after a few years and flourished again until Edward I expelled all Jews from England 100 years later.

THE COUNTRYSIDE

When is a forest not a forest? The hapless folk of Yorkshire lost more of their freedoms when William the Conqueror (who was said to love stags as if he was their father), designated large parts of England as Royal Forest. The word didn't refer to a collection of trees but to an area subject to a number of restrictions concerning the management of deer. It might contain villages and farmland or be treeless moorland or heath; only a relatively small part of it would be forest as we know it.

In a Royal Forest the inhabitants were forbidden to enclose extra land, cut trees or fence their crops against deer. Rights to keep animals on common land or feed pigs in autumn acorn woods had to be paid for. The front toes of peasant dogs had to be cut off to keep them from chasing deer. Numerous Forest laws listed crimes 'against the venison' (i.e. any game animals or birds, including boar) or 'against the vert' (the vegetation), and the Forest Courts that tried infringements could inflict a range of severe penalties (including blinding and mutilation). Quite soon, however, the payment of fines instead of punishment became common because it was more lucrative. In fact, such fines provided a much-needed royal revenue stream, and kings after William created more and more Royal Forests.

Why deer? They were no longer a main source of food and no matter how fond kings were of hunting, they did not personally hunt in most of their Royal Forests (there were far too many). Being something that only a privileged few could own made venison a status symbol; it was prized at banquets and given away by kings to keep fractious nobles sweet. Ruling was a hard and dangerous job. Norman kings could not afford to sit idly in palaces: they had to be actively demonstrating their power. The ability to give generous gifts was one of the ways to do it. Because he had to travel all around the kingdom, the king would send word, often weeks ahead, to the royal huntsmen in the forest nearest to where he was due to stay and command that so many deer be ready for his arrival. The big feasts at Christmas or Pentecost were particularly good times, not just to eat but to give away venison.

Of course, the great lords also aspired to possess their own deer parks, paying the king, to whom all the land nominally belonged, for a licence to enclose one. In Yorkshire many of these private forests were created, as well as royal ones. Their laws must have been a considerable annoyance to local people, providing, as they did, the opportunity for gangs of officious forest administrators to descend from time to time like locusts and squeeze fines out of them.

On the North York Moors were the large forests of Pickering and Spaunton; in the Dales, the forests of Wensleydale, Swaledale, Arkengarthdale and Bardon. In

Nidderdale was the forest of Knaresborough, 20 miles long and 8 miles wide. Further south there were several deer parks around Sheffield and all the land between the Ouse and Derwent was Royal Forest. The forest of Galtres was one of the most productive of royal venison, probably because it was near York where kings often stayed (a per-ambulation in 1316 revealed that by then it consisted of 100,000 acres and contained sixty townships).

Other changes to country life were more beneficial. Watermills for grinding corn (grains like wheat or barley, not sweetcorn) increased greatly in number, making the production of flour much easier. The first windmill in the area appeared at Weedley near South Cave. Cloth-fulling mills, which felted woollen cloth with water-driven hammers instead of the stamping of peasant feet, were also introduced – a foreshadowing of the great industrial cloth industry of the future.

It seems that about this time rabbits were brought into England. The Romans had probably introduced them, but their rabbits, being Mediterranean beasts, appear to have died out. Norman rabbits were carefully nurtured in protected warrens; they were rare and highly prized for meat and fur. The East Riding had ideal dry conditions for the building of these warrens, and rabbits were to become an important product.

YORKSHIRE FOLK:
William of Newburgh: Augustinian canon and historian. William is an important source for details of the Anarchy of Stephen, an account of which can be found in his *History of English Affairs*. He is also a useful teller of early stories about revenants and vampires.

PLACES TO VISIT:
St Cedd's Crypt at Lastingham church, Lastingham, North Yorkshire Moors
Ripon: to see the layout of a Norman town around the market place
Conisbrough Castle: a very good example of a Norman Keep

9

PLENTY AND DISASTER, TWELFTH–FOURTEENTH CENTURIES

By the beginning of the thirteenth century the innovations of Norman rule had bedded in. Norman lords still spoke French rather than English and visited their estates in Normandy, but the peasants (to give them their French name) had started to get used to their overlords and were benefitting from improved markets, new mills, ports and bridges.

Then, in 1206, the French King Philip II captured Normandy from King John. The Normans in England now had a dilemma: they either had to pay homage to the French king for their lands in Normandy or try to get them back by fighting. Either way had expensive consequences. For many, especially those whose lands in England were richer or more extensive than those in France, it was easier to make the best of a bad job and focus on making a life in England, where they concentrated on trying to curb the power of the king. Both King John (who was forced to sign Magna Carta) and Henry III (who was forced to agree to holding a parliament) had their work cut out dealing with rebellions (and a French invasion), but that was mostly down south; in Yorkshire, despite the continued Scottish raiding, things were relatively peaceful and even prosperous.

FARMING

Europe had been enjoying a 400-year period of warmer weather, which had improved the scanty crop yields. More food meant more people survived the winter. The population was growing and with it the need to bring more land into cultivation. In Yorkshire large numbers of cottagers were farming less than 5 acres. Extra land meant that they could avoid splitting up these few acres – hardly enough to feed a family already – to provide for their sons. Woods were felled, forest laws infringed and hitherto unused land brought under the plough. Whether it was in the North York Moors, the stony slopes of the Pennines (where their lynchets – terrace walls – can still be seen), or the High Wolds, land-hungry peasants laboured to increase their holdings. They had the good fortune of being less burdened with feudal obligations to labour for their lords than serfs down south and by the twelfth and thirteenth centuries most could discharge them by paying rent instead. Owners of land improved by their tenants were only too pleased with the additional rents.

Farming was a communal activity, no matter how much land you farmed. People, rich and poor, lived much more communally than we do today: privacy was hard to find and little valued, even thought of as a monkish oddity. Much land was not farmed individually but incorporated into the two or three big common fields of the village, one of which would be allowed to lie fallow every so often to rest it. The fields were divided into strips, allotted annually by village elders, to include good and bad land. Villagers also had rights to keep a certain number of beasts on the common pasture. Communal decisions were made about what was to be grown, when the land was to be ploughed (fields were often ploughed several times before they were sown), and pretty much everything else to do with farming. Ploughs, drawn by oxen, were shared, as were all the tasks of the farming year: sowing, weeding (an endless job in the days before weedkillers), harvesting, threshing, winnowing and, finally, carting the cleaned grain to the mill to be made into flour.

Not all land was farmed in the open field way. Some lords owned vaccaries (cow farms) which raised cows and produced the valuable plough oxen (gelded bulls). Rievaulx and Jervaulx Abbeys both went in for breeding horses, as well as inventing Wensleydale cheese. Because peasants had always been more independent in the Danelaw, there were areas, particularly in the hill and moor regions, where people farmed a few independent acres, or kept their own flocks of sheep (more on this later).

Peasant houses from this period have been excavated in the long-running dig at Wharram Percy in the Wolds. Little changed from those built before the Conquest; they were small, cruck-built long houses divided by a cross passage, with unglazed windows and a central hearth. On one side of the passage lived the family; on the other cattle were over-wintered. A good example can be seen at Ryedale Folk Museum at Hutton le Hole. The walls were built of whatever materials were available locally, mostly wattle and daub. Roofs were slated with stone or thatched.

CASTLES

Their masters continued to live in castles but those who built new ones (having first obtained a licence from the king to 'crenellate', i.e. fortify), wanted the somewhat basic domestic arrangements improved. Men who had seen, on Crusade, the Islamic palaces of the Holy Land wanted some of that comfort in their own castles.

One of the best-preserved castles in Yorkshire is Bolton Castle, built by Sir Henry Scrope at the end of the fourteenth century. Its four great towers, standing around a central courtyard, were impressive enough to deter Scottish raiders but also provided more than seventy rooms for the accommodation of visitors and servants as well as private apartments for the owner and his family.

Sir Henry was not alone in building a grand new castle; other powerful families who were to influence the history of Yorkshire – and England – for the next few centuries also built Yorkshire castles at this time. As well as the Scropes there were the Nevilles at Sheriff Hutton, the Especs at Helmsley, and the Percies at Wressle. These last had risen to power after being given estates in Northumberland as a reward for campaigns against the Scots. Soon they had manors in all three Ridings, including Spofforth, Topcliffe and Pocklington. Only the Duke of Lancaster owned more land in the north.

The ever-present threat of the Scots caused even the lesser nobility to crenellate their manor houses. Markenfield Hall near Ripon is the best existing survivor. Among other security measures it has a moat – a prestigious, if smelly, addition to many manor houses. Flamborough Castle was originally a fortified manor house.

THE WOOL TRADE

'I praise God and ever shall,
It is the sheep hath paid for all!'
(Inscription on a Nottingham merchant's window)

It was during this period that wool production reached its height and became the driving force of the whole economy. Huge flocks of sheep, with their attendant shepherds and dogs, covered many acres of Yorkshire.

Underclothes were mostly made of linen or hemp, but wool was virtually the only material available for outer clothes. It is a very versatile material which can be made into an astonishing range of goods from thick felt to a fine light worsted or a broadcloth almost as smooth as satin (after fulling and knapping).

English wool, thanks to English rain and pasture, grew longer and finer than on the Continent, making it particularly desirable. It was exported to many European countries, some of which relied entirely on English wool for their weavers. Indeed, so popular was it abroad, that

Edward I quickly saw the tax opportunities of the enormous wool sales and slapped a tax on every sack exported (thereby creating a fine career for smugglers). As a result, he was able to finance his wars in both Scotland and France. A more unexpected result was that in order to administer the tax he had to have the co-operation of the great wool merchants of the time, many of whom sat in Parliament, the power of which was thus increased.

At first wool was exported in its raw state, hundreds of thousands of sacks leaving Hull for the weavers of Flanders and Italy. Later on, methods of weaving and dyeing were improved in the county, and finished cloths were exported, adding considerable value to the original product. The short stapled wool of the Dales sheep (the staple is the length of the wool) was woven into a popular hard-wearing coarse cloth called kersey. Longer stapled wool was combed and made into different grades of worsted cloth. A few of the small towns in the West Riding seized the opportunity to begin cloth-making at this time, laying the foundations of their future success.

The job of shepherd was respected all over Yorkshire and a good one much sought after. They were allowed to run some of their own sheep with the lord's herd and were free from doing any extra work for him apart from washing the sheep and shearing. They had certain customary rights too, a bowl of whey all through the summer and the milk of the ewes on Sunday, a lamb at weaning time and a fleece at shearing.

TOWNS

York remained the chief city in the north throughout the Middle Ages, and though it was never as populous as London it was for many years the centre of government when both Edwards I and II lived there, organising their campaigns against the Scots. Parliament (which had to meet wherever the king was) was summoned to meet there many times.

During the thirteenth and early fourteenth century it improved its enclosing walls with four bars (city gates), six posterns (small doors) and sixty-six towers, most of which can still be seen. The eastern side of the city still had no walls but was defended by marshy land, where King's Pool (aka King's Fishpond) is now. The castle was rebuilt in stone and the old keep on the Norman motte where the Jews had met their end was replaced by the clover-leaf-shaped Clifford's Tower.

Beyond the walls the suburbs spread out along the main roads, surrounded by orchards and gardens. Further out still were the common fields that fed a city still reliant to a large extent on locally grown food.

The main conduit for goods was not the muddy rutted roads, but the river Ouse, navigable right up to Boroughbridge. York was a successful inland port, bringing in luxury goods from many places in Europe and exporting lead from the Pennines as well as the inevitable wool. It was now a centre of both secular and ecclesiastical administration and sustained a flourishing collection of craftspeople: leather-workers, pewterers; bell-founders, goldsmiths and glaziers, though most of its tradespeople were connected in some way to the wool trade.

Beverley's fortunes were also dependent on wool, both raw and finished (Beverley 'blue' cloth was a speciality). It even had its own merchants in Bruges to oversee sales, as well as its own resident Flemish weavers, remembered in Flemingate. In those days it was, like York, an inland port. Goods were ferried up Beverley Brook to the river Hull and on to the Humber.

Beverley was also famous for having curious Sanctuary laws. Sanctuary, originally invented to reduce lawless revenge killings, could be claimed in any church by those who were accused of committing a crime. They could stay in the church, provided with food and drink, for thirty days while priests tried to negotiate with their accusers. In Beverley the thirty-day period was extended to three months and the sanctuary-claimer had the freedom of the whole town, providing he or she stayed within the four boundary crosses (three of which still remain). This made Beverley very popular with criminals, who, if found guilty eventually, could be escorted to the conveniently close coast and put on a ship.

Wyke, the town founded by the monks of Meaux, was renamed Kingston-on-Humber by Edward I when he bought the manor. It had its fortunes considerably enhanced by its new lord who enlarged the quay, improved the roads, extended the markets and established a mint. From the beginning it was always aggressively competitive with other ports and exploited its position at the mouth of the Humber to dominate shipping trade.

In 1321, menaced by the Scots, the burgesses obtained a licence to build a massive city wall in brick. Hull was particularly dependent on the wool trade and was home to Richard and William de la Pole, the richest wool merchants and moneylenders in England, whose family were to play an important part in the Wars of the Roses. The merchants of York, Beverley and Hull had more experience of and connections with the towns abroad than any other place in Yorkshire, and their merchants were visited by buyers from all over northern England to haggle for luxuries such as spices and wine.

Yorkshire's fourth richest town was **Scarborough**, its fortunes made by fish, not wool. It is important to understand exactly how important fish were in the Middle Ages. Not just Friday but almost half the days in the year were designated by the Church as fast days, when no meat was to be eaten. (Making fish look like meat was one of the skills of a good cook.) Castles often had fish ponds for fresh fish but even they could not possibly supply enough for a whole year. Instead a huge number of fishermen were employed in catching a huge number of fish, which were salted and carried throughout the land by packmen. Fish was such big business that a disagreement between the Abbots of

St Mary's in York and Meaux over Hornsey Mere fisheries was only finally settled by an expensive dual between their respective champions!

At the mouth of the Humber is Spurn Point, an ever-changing peninsula created by water-deposited stones and sand. In the thirteenth century a similar peninsula was colonised by fishermen. The little villages they built flourished and grew quickly into a sizeable town called Ravenser Odd (the Raven's tongue). Able to entice ships passing up and down the Humber – sometimes in a frankly piratical way – to dock at their port, the inhabitants became rich, and Ravenser Odd at one time rivalled Hull in trade. However, time and tide were against them. First their causeway to the land was washed away, and, by the middle of the fourteenth century, floods and storms caused the inhabitants to move elsewhere as their town disappeared under the waves. 'God's judgement on their evil ways!' said Hulls founders, the monks of Meaux Abbey, piously.

MONASTERIES AND FRIARIES

The thirteenth and fourteenth centuries saw Yorkshire abbeys and priories reach their peak architecturally. This was the great period of English church building, its confidence founded on wealth from wool and heavily influenced by French Gothic design. Thanks to the Dissolution of the Monasteries in the sixteenth century we have, alas, only a fragment of this richness and have to rely on interpretation board drawings to get any idea of the glorious originals.

The new buildings were a sign that the old simplicity of life was disappearing fast; the Cistercians abandoned their original vegetarian diet and their monks sometimes even had small apartments rather than sharing the communal dormitories; Rievaulx flamboyantly flourished new-style additions and Byland got its great Rose Window, deaf to the sound of its founders turning in their humble graves.

The Augustinian Order was no more restrained: Guisborough Priory was rebuilt after a fire with a 352ft-long church with an enormous East Window, while Bridlington Priory acquired a splendid new nave. The recent availability of Florentine credit seems to have meant that a concern with basic economics, never great, went out of the window as far as these grand designs 'for the Glory of God' were concerned; monastic debt soon spiralled out of control. The wool that was supposed to finance the monasteries often had to be given as interest to creditors.

In the late 1220s a new type of religious order, the friars, arrived in Yorkshire. These were men who, following the teachings of St Francis of Assisi, based themselves among the poor in towns, begging like Buddhist monks for a living and preaching to ordinary people, instead of focusing on prayer. There were friaresses in Europe, but the Church was very uncomfortable with them.

There were four orders of friars: the Dominicans (Black Friars, Friar Tuck's order) were the first, then came the Franciscans (Grey Friars, dedicated to absolute poverty), the Carmelites (White Friars) and the Augustinians (Austin Friars). All had friaries in York and many other Yorkshire towns. Being in prime town sites, little remains of any of them, except for the Grey Friars tower in Richmond.

In their day friars were well supported and appreciated by local people, but being so much in the public eye they were vulnerable to accusations of misconduct, and as time passed those who were supposedly wedded to 'My Lady Poverty' got a reputation for immorality. Chaucer's Friar Huberd in *The Canterbury Tales* is delightfully worldly, arranging marriages for young women (with the implication that he was responsible for the necessity), mixing with innkeepers rather than lepers, his tippet stuffed with knives and pins to give to 'yonge wyves'.

> 'Hise eyen twynkled in his heed aright
> As doon the sterres in the frosty nyght.'

ARCHITECTURE

Some of the most beautiful religious buildings in Yorkshire were built at this time, thanks to the increasing wealth and relative peace. Most of these are churches or abbeys with foundations that had the money to employ good masons and buy the best materials.

The Normans, like the Romans, had used round arches to support the weight of their stone buildings (the crypt of York Minster has decorated Norman piers in it that give an idea of the style at its best) but in the twelfth century a new French design of arch revolutionised building. It was discovered that a pointed arch distributed the weight of the walls and roof better. This meant that arches could be thinner and airier. Tall windows supported by these arches could be inserted into the walls and the whole building made lighter and more graceful. The massive Norman pillars were replaced with elegant groups of thinner ones, often of Purbeck marble. This style, known as Gothic, was quickly taken up by the different monastic orders, which were as susceptible to fashion as any other group.

Ripon Cathedral, Beverley Minster and the now partially ruined Howden collegiate church were all rebuilt in the new style, as was York Minster, the glory of Yorkshire. Rivalry with his fellow archbishop (who had just built the cathedral at Canterbury) inspired Walter de Gray, archbishop of York from 1215, to order the building of a new Gothic cathedral in 1220. It was not finished until the fifteenth century: making a cathedral for the glory of God was a slow business! York Minster's glories include the extraordinary West Window and the wonderful East Window in the Lady Chapel, the largest expanse of mediaeval stained glass in the world.

In the East Riding, the most prosperous part of the county at the time, many fine parish churches were rebuilt: St Augustine's at Hedon, Holy Trinity in Hull and, the most beautiful of all, St Patrick's at Patrington.

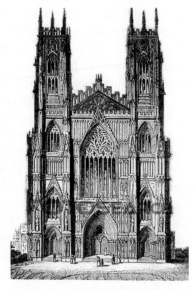

The North and West Ridings were poorer and so have few large Gothic buildings, but even so local churches sometimes managed to add Gothic features, new windows in the nave, perhaps, or additional aisles.

LITERACY, LITERATURE, NAMES

By the fourteenth century the Norman aristocrat's prejudice against reading ('it's a job for priests!') had more or less died out. Although French was still widely spoken at court and schools of French were popular with the growing middle class, it was no longer used in Parliament and even the most aristocratic could speak and read English perfectly well when they wanted to. This trend was greatly enhanced by writers like William Langland (author of *Piers Plowman*) and Geoffrey Chaucer who wrote in the English known as Middle English. Chaucer's *The Canterbury Tales*, witty and vivid descriptions of pilgrims telling stories while on a pilgrimage to St Thomas à Becket's shrine in Canterbury, are still read and enjoyed in modern versions (or even more so by those prepared to put in a bit of time understanding the original language). The same is true of *Sir Gawayne and the Grene Knight*, written in alliterative verse in a slightly more difficult north-western dialect. The language of these stories is sinewy and lively, a delight to anyone who enjoys words.

It was Chaucer, well known at court, who made writing in English respectable and many writers followed him. One of the most popular books of the Middle Ages, *The Prick of Conscience*, was probably written by a Yorkshireman, the hermit Richard Rolle of Hampole, near Doncaster. Quotes taken from its account of the 'Fifteen Signs of Doom' can be seen in the early fifteenth-century stained glass of All Saints' church, in York's North Street.

Several English chronicles were also written in Yorkshire and the very fact that they were not in Latin (as churchmen would expect) shows how reading and the use of books was spreading to ordinary people. Illiteracy was still the norm, but the opportunities for those who could read were no longer just for ordained people; lords needed accountants, secretaries and literate managers; ambitious merchants could now see that educating their sons (usually not their daughters, alas) might give the whole family an advantage.

The dialect spoken in Yorkshire was much more influenced by Scandinavian languages than further south and southern travellers to the north often complained of the 'barbarous' nature of the natives' language, arrogantly assuming that their own was the 'proper' way of speaking. Again it was Chaucer who was the first writer to attempt, in 'The Reeve's Tale' to reproduce the speech of northern folk. A much later version of northern dialect – and a northern view of southerners – can be found in the York and Townley Corpus Christi plays, particularly in the latter's Second Shepherd's Play in which one of the characters, the rascally Mak, is told to 'tak out that southron toothe' (i.e. stop lying!).

This was also the period when the use of surnames became common. People with the same Christian name had probably always been distinguished by adding that of their fathers (John Tom's son, Matthew James' son) or by some other characteristic: James the Butcher, Andrew the Strong Man etc. Now, because of greater movement of people, you might, if you moved to another village to work, be known instead by the name of your old town or village, for example John of Hull, or Peter of Millington.

In the West Riding, where scattered farmsteads were more common than villages, people might be distinguished by the name of their farms: Hebblethwaite, Crabtre, Ackroyd (royd = a clearing), Murgatroyd, Sutcliffe. It is still easy to find in Yorkshire families with names that go back to their Yorkshire ancestors. (In Pocklington, for example, there are people whose surname is Pocklington!) The apple often hasn't fallen far from the tree.

FAMINE

Rapid population growth was brutally halted in the early fourteenth century when, possibly due to the eruption of Mount Tarawa in New Zealand, the warm period came to an abrupt halt all over Europe. 1315 was a year like no other; the skies opened and it rained from May until the autumn. Under the cold leaden sky wheat couldn't ripen, and the hay that sustained animals through the winter was ruined.

With the scarcity food prices began to rise sharply; soon they were beyond the pockets of ordinary folk. The normal low yield of crops meant that famine was always only a harvest away. Villages kept back seed grain for replanting, but there was not usually enough food produced to store much more. Only the rich could afford to hoard large amounts of grain. What little there was now had to be eked out with the time-honoured famine resource of the peasant, wild food: edible roots and plants, nuts, seeds and, in the last resort, grass and bark and earth.

The weather was nearly as bad in the two years following 1315. The famine continued. Desperate people had to slaughter their plough oxen and eat their seed grain, sacrificing their future to the urgent present. Children were abandoned (like Hansel and Gretel), old people starved themselves for the survival of the next generation; even cannibalism was recorded. In Yorkshire matters were made worse by great storms, which destroyed parts of the east coast. The towns of Holon and Hyth were lost, and many acres of productive land disappeared forever into the sea.

The height of the famine was reached in 1317, after which the weather returned to its normal pattern, though it was never quite as benign as before, but the population had been severely weakened and disease easily took hold of both humans and animals. In 1319–20 a cattle plague which had been raging in the south broke out in the north, further reducing food supplies. It is thought that up to 70 per cent of the cattle which had survived the earlier famine were affected. A sheep murrain (disease) had already decimated the flocks. The king was forced to grant massive tax reliefs in the six northern counties including Yorkshire. In the North Riding many communities had their tax assessment lowered by a half and by 1341 more than eighty settlements were still uncultivated. Other parts of Yorkshire were a little better, but overall the rural economy had contracted considerably.

THE BLACK DEATH

In 1348 just when people thought that the worst was over, the Black Death swept across the land with devastating speed. Whether it was bubonic plague, or some deadly virus is now debated, but its effects are not. Somewhere in the region of between a third and a half of the population in Europe died. Mortality rates varied, with some lucky – or blessed – places escaping altogether. Details of what happened in Yorkshire are hard to find, mainly because there was a complete breakdown of ordinary life. We can only imagine the horror and fear of the town-dwellers as their neighbours fell like flies, or the desperation of country dwellers trying to get the harvest in with so few helpers. Even after it began to burn itself out, outbreaks of the Plague continued throughout the fifteenth century.

Its long-term results were stark. At Meaux Abbey only ten of the forty-two monks survived. In Nidderdale forty per cent of holdings were left empty, with many other places hit nearly as badly. Some settlements seem to have been abandoned altogether, and others, like Cowlam, set on an unstoppable path of decline. (It must be pointed out that most of the 375 abandoned villages in Yorkshire are the result of later changes in land use, not the Black Death.)

The saying that every cloud has a silver lining certainly applied to those who had the good fortune to survive the Black Death, because the high mortality benefitted them considerably. No longer did the survivors have to scrape a

living on impoverished stony hillsides as huge amounts of land were suddenly freed up. Rents had, of necessity, been lowered as landlords realised they couldn't get blood out of a stone. On the contrary, they now had to pay higher wages to attract the few people left to work for them. For the first time there was a seller's market in labour. Many of the surviving wealthier peasants were able to buy up more land and become freeholders, founding dynasties of sturdy independent yeoman farmers that were to become the backbone of Tudor England.

On a less positive side, landlords began to understand that there was a commercial advantage in having fewer peasants because they could enclose the open fields and convert them to more lucrative cattle or sheep pasture. Enclosure started in Yorkshire long before its heyday in the eighteenth century. Even though a village like Wharram Percy was badly affected by the Black Death, the villagers actually left in the sixteenth century when its lord converted it into sheep pasture.

WAR WITH SCOTLAND

It was at this moment, when the population was at its most vulnerable, that politics and the inept son of a strong king led to further disaster for Yorkshire and the north.

Edward I was an ambitious ruler, greatly influenced by stories of King Arthur (believed at the time to have been a real king). He decided to enlarge his kingdom by conquering Wales and Scotland. After a successful campaign in Wales and having begun to build the Welsh castles for which he was to become famous, he turned his attention north.

Scotland was in the middle of a dynastic crisis. The Scottish lords asked Edward to help by overseeing their choice of a new king. There were two main claimants, John Balliol and Robert de Bruis, or Bruce (whose Norman family had been given lands in Yorkshire by the Conqueror). Balliol was chosen, but his kingship was soon in trouble and Edward intervened, asserting that he had the right to do so as the Scots, in asking for his help, had accepted him as their feudal lord. At first they went along with this, but when he demanded that they send an army to fight for him against the French, the Scottish lords refused, giving him the excuse he had been looking for. In 1296 he invaded, and so began the First War of Scottish Independence.

He was successful to begin with, capturing Berwick and dominating much of the lowlands, but soon the country rose in rebellion, led initially by Andrew de Moray and William Wallace. There is no room here to tell the full story of the war but things went badly for the Scots. Wallace was captured and executed and when Robert Bruce (originally on Edward's side) stepped forward to claim the throne he was driven into hiding and his forces scattered.

Edward was called by some the Hammer of the Scots but he died in 1307 without capturing Bruce. His son, another Edward (king from 1307–1327), was not the man to carry out his father's plan of conquest. Bruce now began a brilliant guerrilla campaign. Aided by Scots who flocked to him secretly, he systematically captured and then destroyed, one by one, the castles that supported English power. By 1314 only one Scottish town, Stirling, was still in English hands, and it was being besieged by Robert's brother. The defenders agreed with the Scots that if the English did not relieve the town by midsummer it would surrender. Edward II, who had never been very interested in Scotland and who had been having pressing baron problems at home, was stung into action and raised a sizeable army. Bruce, with his much smaller army, never risked open battle if he could help it, but in this case his hand was forced. The English met the Scots at the Bannock Burn near Stirling and, thanks partly to superior Scottish generalship and partly to the marshy ground that bogged down their cavalry, the English were roundly defeated. Edward II was forced to make an undignified escape from the scene, leaving the soldiers

(many of whom would have been Yorkshiremen) to find their own way home, pursued by revengeful Scots.

Bruce now turned the tables, invading and devastating the virtually undefended north, partly as personal revenge (his wife had been imprisoned, his brother beheaded and his sister Mary kept in a cage for four years by Edward's father) and partly to force Edward to acknowledge him as rightful king of Scotland.

Year after year during 'the fighting season', Scottish raiders, led by a man known as the Black Douglas, streamed over the border. They burnt crops, stole livestock and captured men and women for ransom. All people could do was to retreat into the relative safety of towns, leaving the Scots to roam as they pleased. Churches and monasteries were too wealthy to be spared. The rich Cistercian abbeys of North Yorkshire were particularly badly hit; Fountains and Jervaulx were damaged in reprisal for the sacking of Melrose Abbey in Scotland. In 1318 the Scots plundered Ripon and it was only saved from being burnt to the ground by the massive payment of £600. In ten years they had extorted some £20,000 in ransoms alone.

In the same year that Ripon was ransomed the Scots captured the strategic town of Berwick, and, despite – or perhaps because of – his troubles with his rebellious lords (particularly the Duke of Lancaster), Edward was once again forced to act the war leader and try to recapture this key town. While he was besieging Berwick his queen, Isabella, remained at York. Bruce, preferring strategy to war as usual, sent a large body of soldiers into Yorkshire to attempt to capture the queen. She managed a narrow escape to Nottingham with her entourage, but with its soldiers away at Berwick, York itself was unprotected.

The archbishop at the time was a man called William Melton, and it fell to him to organise whatever scant defences could be found in the city. For some reason it was decided not to remain in safety behind the city's walls but to take the fight to the enemy. Melton set about mustering an army of sorts, led by John Hotham, Chancellor of England, and Nicholas Fleming, the Mayor of York. Fighting men they had few; the bulk of the army was made up of people in holy orders, monks, priests, lay brothers, folk who had never fought before but who were willing to risk their lives to defend their city. On 20 September 1319 the brave but doomed army marched out to meet the Scots, whom they understood to be near the River Swale. At Myton-on-Swale, the Scots lay hidden in the smoke from three huge fires and so the English crossed the river in search of them. Then, to their horror, the Scots rushed out of the smoke, surrounding and trapping the small army between the bridge and the water. The archbishop escaped but most of his men, including the mayor, were killed or drowned. Piles of dead men, many in their white religious habits, lay along the shore or floated down the river.

> Alas for sorrow, for there was slain many men of religion and seculars and also priests and clerks...and therefore the Scots called it 'the White Battle'. (*Brut or the Chronicles of England*, ed. F.W.D. Brie, 1906)

The news of the battle forced Edward to abandon his siege, but one piece of good luck for him came out of this disaster: the Duke of Lancaster was accused of betraying the queen's location to the Scots. This gave Edward an excuse to attack the Duke, who had been a considerable thorn in his side, which he did at the Battle of Boroughbridge, proving victorious for once. The troublesome Duke was executed.

The Scottish wars dragged on. Finally in 1322, Edward, determined to finish things one way or another, invaded Scotland with a huge army, made up mostly of vengeful northeners. Once again guerrilla tactics won the day. Bruce, as usual, refused to meet the English in open battle, but retreated before them, burning any available supplies as he went.

Edward pursued, but the further he was drawn into Scotland the more his army's supplies diminished. The ships he was expecting to resupply the army did not appear and things quickly fell apart. Dysentery was already rife and now the army began to starve. Unable to bring his enemy to battle and with his force disintegrating, Edward was once more forced to retreat, hotly pursued by the Scots, who very nearly caught him at Scotch Corner. Having plundered Byland, the Scots found time to take advantage of their proximity to Rievaulx to plunder there as well. Edward fled to Bridlington, still pursued by the Scots, who burnt Bridlington Priory, and thence (via Burstwick) to York, with the Scots still snapping at his heels. It was only when he got into York that they gave up and retired, burning as they went.

In 1327 Edward was deposed (and probably murdered) by his wife Isabella and her lover Mortimer. Her son, the new young King Edward III, was persuaded by nobles grown weary of the Scottish wars to give Bruce what he wanted and acknowledge Scotland as an independent kingdom. The Scots paid a handsome compensation for the raids, but you can be sure that little of it ever reached those who had taken the brunt of them.

The peace treaty didn't stop the raiding on both sides of the border, which continued sporadically in the time-honoured way, but raids seldom came far enough south to trouble Yorkshire seriously again.

THE PEASANTS' REVOLT

'When Adam delved and Eve span, who then was the gentleman?'
(From a sermon of John Ball, radical priest)

The horror of the famine and the Black Death deeply affected the people of England. The ordered world into which they had been born had broken down. Things had changed irrevocably and, as is often the case with change, anger and resentment followed. Neither the prayers of the church, nor the power of their lords had been able to save them, so what was the point of either? With survival came a strong desire for a better life, a wish that for most people was no more than an unattainable dream, but for others brought thoughts of rebellion.

There were two factors that finally sparked revolt. One was the attempt of Parliament (members of which were mostly wealthy landowners or burgesses) to halt the continuing considerable rise in wages by imposing draconian legislation to return it to pre-plague levels. The other was the imposition of a series of poll taxes. 'Poll' means 'head': it was a tax payable by every adult and was intended to finance the ongoing war with France (the Hundred Years' War). Most of the serious rebellion took place down south, where, in June 1381, a sizeable rebel army determined to force the teenage king, Richard II, to lower taxes, put an end to serfdom and get rid of unpopular Officers of State, broke into the Tower of London, where they murdered the Lord Chancellor and the Lord High Treasurer. News of their actions spread throughout the country and in some places there were sympathetic uprisings such as those in Beverley, Scarborough and York.

There is no obvious causal relationship between the southern and northern risings. The northern rebels were not impoverished peasants but well-off townsmen with particular personal grudges against those who ran their towns. It seems to have been the general state of unrest that provided people with the opportunity to express grievances that they might otherwise have kept secret.

In Yorkshire the rising wealth of certain individuals had given them an exclusive position and power within their towns that was resented by those who felt themselves to be just as good. The violence that occurred in the three towns was mostly limited to breaking into the houses of various civic administrators, seizing them, roughing them up a bit, and forcing them against their will to sign bonds swearing to pay their captors certain sums of money. In Beverley the whole twelve-man administrative elite were sacked and replaced by a triumvirate. In York, for some reason, attacks were also made on the Dominican friary.

Although there were death threats, a bit of old-fashioned theft and the scaring of citizens, nothing really unpleasant happened – unless you count the forced parading of one of the king's hated bailiffs around Scarborough to the threatening cry of 'hountays!' (the modern equivalent would be something like 'Party! Party!').

The Earl of Northumberland, Henry Percy, was tasked with sorting out the northern rebels. Commissions were set up to enquire into events, but, as is so often the case with commissions, little clarity emerged. The towns involved were all heavily fined, the status quo was reinstated, and the extorted bonds cancelled. The rioters, as far as we can tell, were fined and pardoned.

AFTERMATH

Amazingly enough, despite its disasters – or perhaps because of them – Yorkshire was flourishing by the end of the fourteenth century. The wider effect of the Peasant's Revolt was that the poll tax was dropped, and the attempt to reintroduce serfdom quietly forgotten. The Black Death had put an end to the feudal laws that forbade peasants from moving from their land. People began to travel about within their own 'country', sometimes swapping farming life for new opportunities in the towns, sometimes finding better pay in other villages. It was still unusual to travel outside a 20-mile radius of where you were born (wayside robbers were common and roads terrible), but occasionally a group of people would get together to see more of the world and visit some holy place on pilgrimage. A new class of people with greater freedom and wealth was arising; they wanted more for their families and were going all-out to get it.

YORKSHIRE FOLK:
Margaret Kirkby: Anchoress of Ravensworth in North Yorkshire. She was the follower of Richard Rolle, the mystic. She was enclosed (shut in a hermitage built into the church wall) first at East Layton and then at Aiderby. Her aim was to experience 'canor', the mystical ecstasy that Rolle taught came from the solitary life of prayer and contemplation.

PLACES TO VISIT:
St Patrick's Church: Patrington
York Minster: York
Rievaulx and **Jervaulx Abbeys**

10

THE LATER MIDDLE AGES, 1400–1485

THE PIRATE WAR

Throughout the Middle Ages English trade with Flanders was extremely important to both countries. Flemish weavers needed English wool to make their superior cloth, and their blacksmiths needed our coal. We wanted not just their beer, soap, salt fish and bronzeware, but also their bricks, which were in more common use there than here. The North Sea was crowded with fishing boats and merchant ships sailing back and forth between ports on the east coast and the Low Countries.

Life at sea was dangerous and hard. If you encountered a boat or ship obviously weaker than your own the temptation to take its goods was great, especially if you knew that their captain would do exactly the same to you should positions be reversed. Professional piracy didn't really exist, but opportunistic piracy certainly did and these temporary pirates were not gentlemen. Chaucer says of his Shipman in *The Canterbury Tales* (modern translation):

'If, when he fought, the enemy vessel sank
He sent his prisoners home by sea: they walked the plank!'

It is difficult to get to the bottom of the serious enmity between east coast fishing towns such as Whitby, Scarborough and Hull, and their counterparts in Flanders, which set off a pirate war in the early fifteenth century. Whether it was fishing rivalry (like the 'Cod War' of the 1970s) or some unrecorded outrage, the tit-for-tat capture of vessels was sufficiently serious to involve the governments of both countries, the prosperities of which largely depended on good trading relationships.

The Hundred Years' War between England and France was still dragging on, and although Richard II had agreed a truce with France, his subsequent murder and replacement by the Lancastrian King Henry IV had rendered it void, so there may have been some national enmity. However, although Flanders was nominally a dominion of France, and although its rulers, the Dukes and Duchesses of Burgundy, tended to side with France, the three wealthiest wool towns, Bruges, Ypres and Ghent unwilling to upset trade, sided with England, a fact which makes the Pirate War even more unexpected.

Whatever the causes, the results were reported in angry complaints and counter-complaints sent backwards and forwards between the two governments.

One of the worst attacks was in May 1402 when an unarmed Flemish fishing boat from Ostend was attacked by a Richard Bric of Hull. In the report he drowned all the sailors and one of the two 'children' on board (probably teenagers, not tots). The ship was then carried off to Scarborough where its 192 barrels of herring and 200 'great fish' were stolen, along with the sea chests, clothes and other possessions of the crew. Henry IV ordered that the ship and the crew be released (it appears that rumours of their murder had been greatly exaggerated and they had only been imprisoned). Although the king's orders were obeyed and the prisoners released, the unlucky crew appear to have been mysteriously murdered on the way home.

Reprisals followed with Flemish fishermen attacking English shipping, particularly ships from Scarborough, although their crews were prudently spared for ransom. The stern intervention of Duchess Margaret of Burgundy, forbidding piracy throughout her realm, had little effect it would seem, because two pirates from Nieuwpoort captured the *Katherine*, the *Rudeschipe* of Scarborough and the *Saint-Maryboat* of Scarborough, as well as another ship in the same year. Some of the sailors were ransomed and some 'horribly drowned'. This is just one example of the increasing North Sea piracy: more followed in the next two years.

In August 1404 things worsened (by this time piratical activities had become widespread in other maritime areas of England and France). 'A great multitude' of English raiders landed at the Flemish town of Wulpen, demolished the church and plundered the inhabitants. At the end of August, a Flemish revenge attack by night captured 'a number of poor fishermen of the north ports', including two from Hornsea. They also captured the Bishop of Hereford, just returning from his investiture in Rome, throwing his crew overboard and holding him for ransom.

In 1405, perhaps because the Bishop had been Henry IV's personal confessor or perhaps because he had just got fed up with all the complaints, Henry sent the main English royal fleet (supposedly 100 ships, but that may be an exaggeration) out to capture the Flemish town of Sluys. It cruised along the Flemish coast, striking fear into its inhabitants. Unfortunately for the expedition, Sluys had recently been re-fortified and so after a siege of five days and heavy losses the fleet returned with little achieved.

In the same year Flemish and Breton pirates attacked and burned Hornsea, 'but the men of Hull, having armed seven ships, pursued them and took them all so that not a single one of them escaped. And they dragged them all to Hull with all the plunder they had taken and their ships, sixteen in number' (translated from the Latin by Dr Charles Kightly).

In the end financial considerations prevailed and the worst of the piracy petered out under pressure from both governments, though, like Border raiding, it never really stopped. The fishermen of the East Yorkshire coast returned to their usual trade, but they retained a certain toughness and dislike of laws.

THE WARS OF THE ROSES BEGIN

> Misrule doth rise and maketh neighbours war
> John Hardyng, chronicler

Forget the roses, forget the cities of York and Lancaster, forget noble knights fighting for the rightful heir to the throne: this nasty collection of betrayal, treason and slaughter boils down to a series of feuds fought out between powerful families. Skirmishes were many but pitched battles much fewer and farther apart than the famous Shakespeare plays imply.

The whole conflict was sparked off by a quarrel between the two most powerful northern families, the Percys and the Nevilles; it continued, off and on, for the best part of thirty years until Richard III, the last Yorkist king, was killed at the Battle of Bosworth. We do not need to follow the intricate twists and turns of the whole story because much of it took place outside Yorkshire, and yet it started here, and it was here in Yorkshire that the largest battle ever fought in Britain took place at Towton.

Although it was the northern feud that started the war, the main underlying cause was the weakness of the ruling king, Henry VI. His grandfather, Henry of Bolingbroke, cousin of Richard II, had usurped and murdered his cousin, claiming the throne as Henry IV by right of his descent from Edward III.

Henry Bolingbroke's son, the glorious Henry V, had stabilised the country and was the sort of strong king the English nobles needed to keep them in order. Unfortunately for England, Henry died when his son, another Henry, was only a baby. Long regencies tended to spell trouble for a kingdom as nobles, unrestrained by the usual stern oversight of a ruler, jostled for influence over the hapless child. In this case a regency council was appointed which tried to rule conscientiously in the baby's name, but failed to prevent certain lords acquiring more power than was safe.

All this took place at a time when the revenues of both king and nobles were considerably reduced by the great rise in agricultural wages (the peasants, for once, were having a happy time), a slump in trade and the loss of valuable lands in France. Lack of financial understanding appears to have been the curse of the aristocracy for many centuries: it was considered ignoble to be always penny-pinching. Fine clothes and a grand retinue meant everything in this period and the great lords spent vast sums on their own glory while galloping merrily towards insolvency. The king himself, despite reminders which grew ever louder, was quite incapable of believing that his resources were limited. By 1450 he was close to becoming bankrupt.

In a religious and hierarchical society like that of the Middle Ages, faith in the king is axiomatic: he was chosen by God and this was reinforced at his coronation with special holy oil sent by the Pope. If a king proved to be unsatisfactory there was a polite fiction that not he but his evil councillors were at fault. Henry's subjects continued to support him as king no matter how useless he was, but matters were coming to a head. Parliament eventually demanded, and got, the removal of the king's hated chief councillor, William de la Pole, Earl of Suffolk. At the same time another player arrived on the scene, ready, as it was thought, to champion the unhappy people of England. Richard, Duke of York, one of the richest men in England (and, incidentally, the possessor of a claim to the throne possibly as good

as the king's), arrived back from Ireland, determined to curb the king's follies and regain what he considered to be his own rightful place at court. Richard was an active, arrogant and impulsive man who felt himself ignored by the king. He returned determined to persuade the king to change his ways and his councillors. The king, of course, smilingly agreed to his reforms and did absolutely nothing.

Piqued, Richard then made the mistake of an arrogant man and attempted an uprising, hoping to capture the king and make him see sense. Here the conservative nature of medieval society was his undoing. It was one thing to try to reform the court, but quite another to raise rebellion against the king. Finding little support, Richard was forced to sue for the king's pardon and retreated to his own lands.

PERCYS AND NEVILLES

Little of this mattered as yet to the people of Yorkshire. They had their own problems and looked to their own lords for protection: the Percys of Spofforth, Topcliffe, Leconfield and Wressle; the Nevilles of Middleham and Sheriff Hutton; the Cliffords of Skipton; the Scropes of Bolton and Masham. Unfortunately, those lords had fallen out spectacularly.

The Percys, a wild, unruly family, traditionally Dukes of Northumberland, were the Wardens of the Eastern Marches, protecting the east side of the country from the Scots. They had frequently rebelled against the Crown, and though they had recently had their confiscated lands restored, they were short of money and no longer trusted at court. The Nevilles, on the other hand, though comparative newcomers, were the up and coming Wardens of the Western Marches (including Cumbria). Ralph Neville's twelve ambitious and unscrupulous children had married their way into the wealthiest and most important families in England. They were now challenging the Percys for domination of the north.

In 1453 the son of Richard Neville, Earl of Salisbury, married the daughter of Lord Cromwell who was holding Wressle, a former Percy possession. The large marriage party set off home from Wressle only to meet Thomas Percy, Lord Egremont, a violent son of the Duke of Northumberland, waiting for them with a band of something like 800 men. Insults and threats were exchanged but the Neville party, protectively surrounding the new bride and the bridegroom's mother, managed somehow to get back to their castle at Sheriff Hutton without bloodshed.

The Percy gauntlet had been thrown down and the Nevilles took it up. During the next two months gangs of liveried bullies from both sides scoured the countryside attacking each other's supporters. (One man escaped being murdered on the altar of the church he had taken refuge in only when the priest waved the Sacred Host in the face of his attackers!)

Complaints rained in on the king, who sent remonstrations to both sides with demands for their better behaviour, but to no avail.

By October both the Percys and the Nevilles had gathered private armies of about 10,000 men, mostly tough battle-hardened northerners. The Percys assembled at Topcliffe and the Nevilles 3 miles away at Sand Hutton. For three days battle looked immanent. Yorkshire held its breath.

Then they all agreed a truce and went home.

Modern readers may be surprised (or disappointed) that nothing more exciting happened, but the forces seem to have been pretty evenly matched and so there was no point slugging it out. Battles are unchancy things and soldiers, even ill-paid underfed medieval soldiers, are valuable; the only reason for fighting is that you're trapped, or because you have a lot more men than your enemy. It's not about fairness.

The two sides went away, but nothing had been settled.

CHOOSING SIDES

In August 1453, King Henry suddenly suffered a mysterious shock that resulted in his becoming cataleptic – completely unresponsive. He had never been strong mentally, and the stresses caused by the continuing losses of English lands in France and the squabbling of his lords was too much for him. A protector had to be appointed. His fiery queen, Margaret of Anjou, who had just given birth to the king's first son, put herself forward, but appointing a woman was a step too far for the king's councillors. They turned to the man who was probably next in line for the throne, Richard, Duke of York. Suddenly he was back at court, his prospects rosy.

Up in Yorkshire Thomas Percy, Lord Egremont, had found a new ally, the vicious and stupid Henry Holand, Duke of Exeter, who had a distant claim to the throne. His motivation is not very clear, but Thomas appears to have wanted to create a coup to put Holand on the throne.

The two men met up in York city and called upon all and sundry to join them. York was going through a bad time: its wool trade had declined because of competition from the towns of West Yorkshire. Men of all trades were out of work, and young men were finding it hard to get apprenticeships. Thomas found many disaffected souls willing to join him. However, the projected coup did not get far. When Exeter rode south to raise men in his own lands few responded, and before long he was chased into taking sanctuary. Thomas Percy raised some troops from the Percy lands around Pocklington, but on his way west he encountered two of the Nevilles with their own men. There was a violent skirmish and the Pocklington men fled, leaving Thomas to be captured. True to his nature he later achieved a daring escape from Newgate gaol, but eventually met a headsman's axe.

Although the Duke of York tried to be even-handed to both Nevilles and Percys as Protector, he couldn't disguise the fact that he really favoured the former. The queen, on the other hand, detested York and so his enemies naturally gathered around her. With the Nevilles supporting the Duke of York it was inevitable that the Percys, headed by the Duke of Northumberland, would support the queen's Lancastrian party.

Then, unexpectedly, the king recovered. Once more York's fortunes were reversed as his job as Protector disappeared and it became obvious that the queen and his enemies were out to get his blood. Summoned to appear before the great council at Leicester he was forced to act. Before the royal party on its way to Leicester could do more than hastily gather a small force, York had raised a larger one and swiftly marched to intercept them at St Albans. Attacking the king's party was a serious risk but the Duke took it. Talks achieved nothing. The town was taken and, in a bloodbath, the Duke of Northumberland, Lord Clifford and the Duke of Somerset, all Lancastrian supporters, were hacked down, the king himself injured and captured.

St Alban's was the first real battle of the Wars of the Roses; its bloodshed produced a hardening of positions, with the more conservative Percys (and most of Yorkshire) supporting the Lancastrian king's party and the opportunistic Nevilles supporting the Duke of York, the new man.

THE QUEEN STEPS IN

Poor King Henry was freed and recaptured several more times, lending a spurious legitimacy to whomever held him, but it was the indomitable Queen Margaret who became the real Lancastrian leader. Determined to preserve the crown for her son, she was quite as ruthless as her enemies.

Both parties had reverses. At one time Margaret was forced to escape to Scotland, at another it was Richard of York who had to flee. It was only a matter of time before the

Duke realised that merely capturing the king did not give him the power he wanted. Despite opposition he claimed the throne for himself.

After considerable debate in Parliament it was agreed that Henry should remain king for his lifetime but that the Duke would become king after Henry's death (Henry's son was thus disinherited).

Margaret, meanwhile, had been gathering troops in the north. She had no intention of allowing Henry to relinquish the throne (although he appears to have been quite happy to do so). In 1461, with the revenge-filled sons of the lords killed at St Albans, she began to march an army south. Richard confidently marched north from London to meet her, spending Christmas at his castle of Sandal, near Wakefield. As Margaret's army approached, he, arrogant as ever, made the fatal mistake of leaving the safety of the castle to attack it. The result was disaster. Historian Edward Hall says: 'he was environed on every side, like a fish in a net, or a deer in a buckstall; so that he, manfully fighting, was within half an hour slain and dead.'

His second son, Edmund, was also killed and Micklegate Bar in York soon had new ornaments, the heads of York and his son, the former adorned with a paper crown on which were the words 'Let York overlook the town of York.'

It seemed to Margaret that she and the Lancastrians had won. All that remained was to re-establish royal control of London. They merrily continued their march south, pillaging as they went like an invading army. Disappointment, however, awaited them in London. The city, panic-stricken and fearing for its riches, shut the gates against them. The Lancastrians were forced to retreat back to Yorkshire, their supplies dwindling. Bad news followed them.

THE BATTLE OF TOWTON

Only 18 years old, but an impressive 6ft 3in tall and with battle experience, the eldest of Richard of York's surviving sons, Edward, was racing across the country to London. After its recent scare the city quickly made its choice and opened its gates to him. The nobles who had opposed his father's claim swiftly agreed that his son should be crowned as Edward IV.

Margaret and Henry had by this time reached the safety of York. The Lancastrian army had grown and was now huge, but Henry was clearly unfit to lead it. Hearing of Edward's coronation and the approach of his avenging army, it was agreed to give command to the Duke of Somerset, who drew up his forces in a good defensive position near York at Towton. He was no doubt pleased to hear that Edward's force was considerably smaller.

In fact, the Yorkist forces were advancing in three armies, one from the west, one via Yorkshire and one supposedly being gathered in the east by the unreliable Duke of Norfolk. Having won a nasty little encounter with Lancastrians at Ferrybridge, the Yorkists reached Towton. Norfolk and his men, however, were still missing, but Edward, with a young man's fearlessness, was not prepared to wait.

As the two sides, close on 50,000 men, readied themselves for battle under dark March skies, unseasonably heavy snow began to fall, driven by strong winds towards the Lancastrian position. Edward's commander, Lord Fauconberg, on seeing this, gave orders to the longbowmen to shoot from their furthest range, allowing the wind to carry the arrows to the enemy while staying out of reach themselves. The Lancastrians' own arrows, shot into the blinding snow, fell short, where they lay conveniently close at hand for the Yorkist bowmen to re-use them. For three hours the two sides fought in terrible conditions without a decisive outcome. Then the tardy Duke of Norfolk and his men arrived and things slowly began to change in the Yorkists' favour.

Eventually the Lancastrian line broke and men began to retreat. In no time the retreat turned into a rout; helmets and armour were thrown off; men trod each other down in the slush as they ran from the slaughterers behind them. Evidence from excavations on the site during 1996 show how violent the battle became: skulls split open with battle-axes, bones showing the marks of multiple stab wounds. Both sides had declared that no quarter should be given, so that even those who surrendered were killed. At the end of the ten-hour battle the victors could hardly lift their bloodstained weapons.

The death toll was huge, in the region of 28,000 men. Edward's risk had paid off and the Lancastrians had lost not just the battle and their soldiers, but a large number of their most important nobles. Henry and Margaret once again escaped to Scotland and until 1470 Edward was able to rule in peace.

TREACHERY AND THE END OF LANCASTER

Edward's reign now appeared assured but in 1470 his main supporter, Richard Neville, Duke of Warwick, known as the Kingmaker, frustrated in his attempts to control the king he felt he had made, suddenly changed sides and made a dubious peace with Margaret. Edward had to flee briefly to Flanders, but he returned the following year, sailing up the Humber to land at Ravenser. Hull, always contrary, refused him entry, but Beverley and York supported him and he went on to kill Warwick at the Battle of Barnet. A month later Edward defeated a Lancastrian army raised by the queen (Henry was being 'kept safe' in the Tower of London by this time). Henry's 18-year-old son was killed in the battle, putting an end to any possibility of Lancastrian rule continuing, and Edward made quite sure that no one else tried ruling through Henry by returning to London and having him murdered. Broken by the death of her son, Margaret returned to France.

From 1475 Edward's brother, Richard, Duke of Gloucester, twelfth of the thirteen children of the dead Duke of York, began to concentrate his lands in the north and built up a power base in his castles at Middleham (where he had been brought up) and Sheriff Hutton. He married Anne Neville, Warwick's daughter, and she brought him a share of the Neville wealth. He was rewarded with other honours and lands by Edward, who appreciated his loyalty and fighting abilities. Most of the Percys being thoroughly out of favour, Richard was able to control the north until Edward's death. He seems to have been popular with local people, especially in York.

In 1472 Edward set up the Council of the North, an important body in the history of Yorkshire. His primary intention in creating it was to improve peace-keeping in the unruly north by settling land disputes, preventing vendettas between landowners, and punishing law-breakers more efficiently than could be done from London. His secondary intention was to promote the well-being of the area by improved government oversight. Richard was made Lord President of the council, which met initially at Sandal Castle four times a year.

Everything changed when Edward unexpectedly died in his early 40s and Richard left Yorkshire for London to become Protector to his brother's two sons (the unfortunate Princes in the Tower) and, eventually, king. But that, as they say, is another story.

A NOTE ON THE NAMES OF LORDS

It is easy to become confused by aristocratic names. Lords all have Christian names (annoyingly often the same as their fathers'), and family names (Percy, Clifford, etc.). They also have titles, some of which may be inherited and some given to them during their lifetime by the king. Histories usually refer to people's title: York, Lancaster, etc., meaning the

Duke of York or Lancaster, but these titles do not necessarily imply that their possessors had any great connection with the places. The Duke of York, for example, did indeed own a few manors in Yorkshire, but the main part of his lands was in the Welsh Marches. The Duke of Lancaster, on the other hand, owned a very large proportion of Yorkshire. Eldest sons usually inherited their father's titles and so were known by the same names; thus, the son of the dead Duke of York is the Duke of York. To make matters more complicated, titles could be taken away and given to completely different people.

YORKSHIRE FOLK:
Archbishop Neville of York: Brother of Warwick 'the Kingmaker', who helped put Edward IV on the throne. At his enthronement as archbishop in 1465 at Cawood Castle there were about 2,500 people to be fed at each meal. They consumed 4,000 pigeons and 4,000 crays, 2,000 chickens, 204 cranes, 104 peacocks, 100 dozen quails, 400 swans and 400 herons, 113 oxen, 6 wild bulls, 608 pikes and bream, 12 porpoises and seals, 1,000 sheep, 304 calves, 2,000 pigs, 1,000 capons, 400 plovers, 200 dozen of a bird called 'rees' (i.e. ruffs), 4,000 mallard and teals, 204 kids and 204 bitterns, 200 pheasants, 500 partridges, 400 woodcocks, 100 curlews, 1,000 egrets, over 500 stags, bucks and roes, 4,000 cold and 1,500 hot venison pies, 4,000 dishes of jelly, 4,000 baked tarts, 2,000 hot custards with a proportionate quantity of bread, sugared delicacies and cakes, and 300 tuns of ale and 100 tuns of wine. (Francis GODWIN, *De Præsulibus Angliae*, ed. Richardson)
Feeling full?

PLACES TO VISIT:
Merchant Adventurers' Hall, York: In the undercroft you can see modern versions of the banners of different guilds illustrated with the tools of their trades

Towton Battlefield: Very atmospheric, especially in the rain
Barley Hall, York: Reproductions of late fifteenth-century rooms in a renovated late fifteenth-century house
Bishops' House: Norton Leeds Lane, Sheffield, South Yorkshire, S8 9BE. Surviving timber-framed house
Bolton Castle, Wensleydale: A well-preserved example of a late medieval castle, property of the Scrope family (open to visitors)
Beverley Minster: An amazing carving at the burial place of the Percys

THE EARLY TUDORS, 1485–1547

TOWNS

When Henry Tudor entered York a year after winning the Battle of Bosworth, he was greeted by cheering crowds, singing children, showers of sweetmeats and rosewater, music and pageants. It was a surprising welcome from a city that had supported the man he had just defeated (Richard III), but the Mayor and aldermen were desperate to gain the new king's favour. The city's fortunes were at rock bottom: its cloth trade had declined and business was bad. Houses were being abandoned and the second city in England was having trouble paying its taxes.

York was not alone. The Europe-wide recession caused by the Black Death continued to affect business in many Yorkshire towns through to the end of the fifteenth century and into the early sixteenth. Not just York but Beverley, Hull and the smaller towns of North and East Yorkshire saw their prosperity decline.

Things were better in the West Riding. Here clothiers were free from the strict York cloth regulations, and there were plenty of fast-flowing becks to power fulling mills. The towns of Rotherham, Bradford, Doncaster, Halifax and Wakefield had taken to cloth-making and were becoming prosperous. There was also an abundance of good clay in the area which, although used since Roman times, was now exploited in an increasingly important pottery industry. While the aristocracy licked its wounds from the wars, these ordinary Yorkshire folk, freed from feudal obligations and with nothing to lose, were enthusiastically exploring opportunities for making money.

A sign of the improved West Riding wealth was the rebuilding of parish churches, such as Bradfield and Ecclesfield, in a new and peculiarly English style of architecture, the Perpendicular, which emphasised vertical lines.

Borrowing was a problem for new businesses and, thanks to Edward I's ban, there were now no Jewish financiers to borrow from. Banks had not yet been invented and a Europe-wide shortage of specie (actual coins) meant that systems of credit had to evolve. One of the most useful was the bond, a document promising that the borrower would pay a named amount to a named person on a particular date (and sometimes even in a named place). The owner of the bond could then use it as collateral or even sell it on. Debts were always difficult to recover, however (some people even left them to their children in their wills), and the many different courts were choked with cases of debt. The law, too, was being forced to evolve to deal with new challenges; this was one of the great periods for lawyers to make their fortune!

London merchants were gradually cornering English trade with France, Italy and Spain, so northern ports such as Hull and the east coast towns began develop ties with places such as Iceland, Scandinavia and Eastland, as northern Germany and the Baltic states were called. Cut-throat competition, especially with the merchants of the powerful Hanseatic League, and the inevitable piracy made such ventures risky, so merchants tended to spread the risk by banding together into trading groups. One such was 'the Merchant Adventurers of the City of York', which grew up out of a religious charity. Its members mostly belonged to the Mercers' Guild (silk merchants). The Adventurers were not out for excitement but were men who 'adventured' their capital in foreign trade. (Women may also occasionally have traded, but only through male relatives.) The company thrived and was able to build the splendid Merchant Adventurers' Hall in York, providing for members who lost their money or fell ill.

As well as regulating trade and protecting their members, York guilds, such as the Mercers, produced the pageants that accompanied the Feast of Corpus Christi. This was a festival (still held in Catholic countries) that celebrated the Blessed Sacrament: the real presence of the flesh and blood of Christ in the bread and wine taken at Communion in the Christian Mass. The Mass emphasises our redemption from sin through Christ's sacrifice at the Crucifixion: the York pageants illustrated the same theme more graphically. They provided a way for those watching to experience the stories underlying the Sacrament, and without which it would have had no meaning. The Doomsday play at the end of the cycle demonstrated in satisfyingly gruesome detail what would happen to those who refused to abandon sin and thus rejected Christ's sacrifice.

Performed on wagons around the city, the series of pageants represented history of the world from the Creation to Doomsday based on texts familiar to all from street preaching and the common annual round of worship. Their origin is debated, but their connection with the city's guilds dates from their beginning, sometime in the early fifteenth century. Each pageant was performed at each of the twelve stations. The onlookers could thus move around at will, watching as God's design unfolded, their faith in the literal truth of the Bible allowing them to identify with the various Biblical characters (played by local men) in a way we cannot now recapture.

Which guild produced which play was sometimes related to a perceived connection with its story; thus, the goldsmiths were responsible for The Three Kings pageant, and the rich Mercers, Doomsday, with its expensive stage machinery for Heaven and Hell and the glorious garments of God and the angels. The butchers' responsibility for representing the Death of Christ may surprise us, but not in an age to which the butchery of execution was familiar. The cost of putting such plays on was considerable but the fact that the guilds continued to find the money for their staging for 200 years says something about their continuing popularity.

COUNTRY

Most people did not live in towns. Even in the West Riding the cloth industry was a rural home business. Sheep farmers took their clip to a town, such as Halifax, and sold it to middlemen to be resold piecemeal to spinners and weavers. These then carried it back to their own homes (often on their own backs), turned it into yarn or, if they were rich enough to own a loom, into cloth, and then carried it back to sell in town. The whole thing was inconvenient and inefficient, but those who did it were their own masters and wealth was distributed more widely than in later centuries. In many hillside villages and farms above the Pennine valleys people now practiced the dual economy of farming and weaving, producing their own wool. Women were an essential part of this economy, spinning the yarn for their husbands to weave.

One of the specialist exports of the West Riding was broadcloth. This was an expensive cloth woven on wider looms requiring several men. It was finished by shrinking that extra width into a dense, warm, almost waterproof cloth by striking it with hammers in fulling mills. It is still used for expensive overcoats, and soldiers' dress uniforms and has a beautiful soft finish with a sheen.

The success of finding additional ways of adding to the income provided by farming led to many new ventures. In Hallamshire a home cutlery industry had existed for a long time (Sheffield knives are mentioned by Chaucer). Ironstone from the Tankersley seam was used for blades and this, combined with easy access to coal for the smithies, suitable stone for grinding edges and swiftly descending becks to provide power for grindstone made Sheffield and the countryside around it an area with increasing fame for metalwork of all kinds. Coal had been used, where available, for hundreds of years. Mostly it was sea-coal, collected from shores where a seam reached the surface; large amounts were transported south in coastal barges. Inland, an outcrop might be mined in shallow pits or adits by whoever found it on his land, but its weight and the lack of good roads and cheap transport made it only useful locally.

The Plague's reduction of the rural population had led many landlords to clear the remaining houses and enclose the arable lands to create a manorial park or sheep pasture. At Allerton Mauleverer, Harewood, Temple Newsam, Norton Conyers, Holme on Spalding Moor, Leconfield and Ribston – the list is long – decaying villages were removed. A government enquiry into enclosure in 1517 showed that, all over Yorkshire, land was being enclosed and families evicted. What happened to them then was, of course, not usually recorded.

It was not just landlords who were enclosing land. Old communal ways of farming were disappearing in some places. By the middle of the sixteenth century many of the small 'townlands' around villages on the edge of the Pennines had been broken up and leased to individual families. Enterprising upland families nibbled away at the moorland edges, often enclosing intakes illegally. Extra land could provide you with enough income to buy a loom and improve your family's life.

HOUSES

Apart from castles, few dwellings earlier than the fifteenth century remain in Yorkshire; the houses of ordinary people have long been swept away or rebuilt. Traditional methods of construction were simple; the commonest and cheapest using crucks infilled with wattle and daub. Crucks were cut from naturally curved pieces of timber which were leaned together to form an inverted 'V'. Pairs of these, fastened together with a ridge-beam, formed a basic frame, the sides of which could then be filled in with walls made of woven withies (willow wands) and plastered with a mix of mud, dung and straw. A building produced in this way used easily found local ingredients and could be adapted to whatever purpose was desired: house, barn, stable, etc.

Those with more money preferred more sophisticated buildings that used box construction: a straight-sided wooden frame supporting a triangular roof section. In towns such as Wakefield and York, where houses were close together and plots small, the upper part of the house might be made larger by being built out over the street – the Shambles in York is a good example. Wattle and daub could be replaced with brick (becoming much more common in this period) or even, for the rich, by stone. Chimneys, or at least wood and plaster smoke-hoods, began to replace the open hearths of the past.

Houses of the Tudor period are often depicted as being white with black beams, but this is a Victorian idea. In fact, the plaster was painted in different colours, depending on what paint ingredients were available locally; often ochre or a soft pink, sometimes with stencilled decorations.

THE MATTER OF RELIGION

Some basic insight into religious feeling is essential for an understanding of the past because so much of our history is bound up with it. At the end of the Middle Ages Christian belief was the solid foundation on which people built their lives. Of course, there were always some who didn't believe, but they kept their heads down, and as far as we know were only a small minority. Even if you weren't particularly religious the stories and the long tradition of church services were like the ground you walked on; the one certainty in a dangerous, uncertain world. During the sixteenth and seventeenth centuries this certainty was damaged and people set at odds with each other in ways that could be both disastrous and beneficial.

It is probable that most people in Yorkshire were only vaguely aware of the new ideas about religion swirling around Germany, the Low Countries and the English court. Criticism of the Church, or more specifically, how it was run, had been common for centuries, but criticism of what it actually taught was much rarer. Few people could read the Bible because it was in Latin. Any interpretation of what it said was a matter for priests.

Henry VII started his reign by rewriting history to make his victory at Bosworth appear the heroic triumph of Good (himself) over Evil (Richard III). He went on to put the country into a better financial state. His son, Henry VIII, inherited a full treasury and proceeded to spend it on enhancing his own importance among the rulers of Europe. His break with the Pope and reinvention as the head of the English Church in 1534 must have come like lightning from a clear sky to ordinary folk, for whom severing ties with the Pope was like severing ties with Christendom itself.

Shortly after Henry's break with Rome new preachers began to enter Yorkshire, teaching things that disturbed many folk. The tenets of Protestantism – the right to read the Bible in your own language and interpret it according to your own conscience and the idea that you could not be saved by your own virtuous actions but only by faith – were seen as heresy in the conservative north. A worse shock was to come in 1536.

By the sixteenth century the fine fervour that had attracted so many people to found monasteries had long died down. The gap between the wealthy foundations such as Fountains and Rievaulx and the small poor ones had widened considerably as numbers of monks and nuns declined. Standards had deteriorated as well because over the years some of those who took the vows of chastity and poverty either ignored or invented ways around them. Their lands and buildings, however, were as valuable as ever.

Henry was running out of money. His chancellor, Thomas Cromwell, came up with the perfect solution. Many monasteries had under-used assets. Who could possibly object if he closed the *smallest* ones and channelled the money into worthier streams? In 1536 the order for the closure of monasteries and nunneries with less than twelve inmates was made. Their monks were to be redistributed or pensioned off.

In the south the effect of this may not have been as great as it was in the much poorer north, where the greatest number of these smaller monasteries were located. Up here, people had always relied heavily on them to care for their aged, sick and poor as well as to maintain the infrastructure of bridges, roads and dykes. Suddenly these things were no one's responsibility any more. For York the closures were particularly devastating as it possessed four monasteries, four friaries, a nunnery and numerous hospitals and chapels maintained by the church.

Rumours, true and false, ran around Yorkshire: the king's devil chancellor, not satisfied with snapping up the smaller monasteries, wanted to despoil the parish churches, steal their silver plate and even tax baptisms. Ordinary people, already confused, became angry. Why would no one listen to them? These so-called reforms had to stop. Widespread resentment at a remote central government quickly turned into rebellion.

The first sign of unrest was an uprising in Lincolnshire in October 1536. It was quickly suppressed, but within weeks rebellion had spread to Beverley, the Wolds and Holderness. Local landlords (whether willingly or by coercion) joined the rebels and chose a leader, a Yorkshire-born London lawyer from Aughton, Robert Aske. He had written a defence of monasteries, saying that they were 'one of the beauties of this realm to all men and strangers passing through'.

On 16 October the now-considerable band of rebels reached York, where the mayor reluctantly allowed them into the city on the grounds that the town was too divided to cope with a siege. The archbishop, together with other senior clerics and some local gentry, took refuge in Pontefract Castle, where the custodian was Lord Darcy. However, as soon as the rebels arrived he surrendered, protesting in a letter to the king that the castle was too decrepit to withstand a siege. Despite his objections he also joined what was now named by Aske 'The Pilgrimage of Grace'. This name emphasised that the rising was not really a rebellion but had a sober religious purpose. Followers of independent uprisings in Riponshire and Richmondshire met up with Aske's forces at Pontefract and together they advanced on Doncaster, more joining them as they went. By the end of October few of the leading Yorkshire families remained loyal to the king and virtually the whole of the north between the Don and the Scottish border was in rebel hands.

What were they hoping to achieve? The Pilgrims had many grievances other than purely religious ones, but this was not an attempt to usurp the throne. They wanted the king to reopen the closed monasteries, reinstate their inhabitants and get rid of those old scapegoat 'evil councillors', particularly the base-born Thomas Cromwell (son of a butcher). To emphasise the purity of their intentions the Pilgrims all took an oath promising to protect the king and to behave well, but also to remove 'these heretics and their opinions'. They marched under a banner depicting the Five Wounds of Christ, rather than military colours, but the threat of well over 20,000 men, however well-behaved, was one that had to be taken seriously. The king's position was weak, so when his appointed representative, the Duke of Norfolk (who had Yorkshire connections and so was trusted by the rebels) met them at Doncaster Bridge, he had a soothing message. The king, he said, promised to hold a parliament in York to hear their complaints, and, in the meantime, Aske was invited to come to see the King in London, to discuss matters with him personally. The Pilgrims, promised a free pardon, naively returned home rejoicing. Aske duly went to London where the king listened to him and even gave him a red silk jacket. Never trust fair words from an autocrat! Within a few months a second revolt gave Henry the excuse to revoke the pardons and the leaders of the Pilgrimage of Grace had been tried, condemned, hanged, drawn and quartered. Aske was executed at York and Sir Robert Constable, another of the leaders, at Hull, 'so trimmed with chains, that his bones will hang there this hundred years', as the treacherous Duke of Norfolk gleefully remarked.

Lord Darcy, Sir Thomas Percy, the priors of Bridlington, Guisborough and the Carmelite friary at Doncaster were also executed, as well as the abbots of Fountains, Rievaulx and Jervaulx. The poor abbot of Jervaulx, who had been forced by his own monks to join the Pilgrimage, left his name scratched on his prison wall in the Tower: 'Adam Sedber Abbas Jorvall [Abbot of Jervaulx] 1537'.

The fear instilled by these brutal punishments silenced any serious opposition when the inevitable happened and the king's commissioners arrived to close the remaining monasteries. Offers of pensions were swiftly accepted as a frenzy of plundering (far worse than anything the Scots had done) began. The king was so short of money that he was prepared to sell off the land and assets to anyone who could produce the cash or offer him a large loan. Lead from the roofs, timber from the estates, the very stone and marble from the walls, all was taken by gentry in favour with the king, some of whom turned monastic buildings into private houses. Even the monastery bells that had sounded out over Yorkshire valleys for centuries were melted down. Rung to mark the various religious offices during the day they, and the sun, had been the only timekeepers for local people.

Whatever remained at the monastic sites was carried away, legally or illegally, by scavengers.

> All things of price [were] either spoiled, carped away or defaced to the uttermost ... it seemeth that every person bent himself to filch or steal what he could.
>
> Michael Sherbrook, rector of Wickerley

By 1540 all the monasteries in England had been closed. As the Protestant Reformation took hold there followed extensive changes to the services and appearance of churches. In 1548 many of the major ceremonies of the church were suppressed as superstitious; saints' images were destroyed (idolatrous!) and altars (pagan!) replaced by communion tables. In Yorkshire many felt that these changes had been foisted on them by a southern elite. Once again fear of royal retaliation prevented any overt objection, but a large number of Yorkshire nobility as well as ordinary people

secretly remained faithful to the old ways. The matter of religion was far from settled.

HENRY VIII'S GREAT PROGRESS

Henry's betrayal of the Pilgrims of Grace provided only a temporary settlement of his northern problems. The situation in the county was getting worse all the time as assets from the closed monasteries disappeared into southern hands. Henry, like many southerners, distrusted and feared the unpredictable north, where people were tough and independent, hardened by years of fighting the Scots as well as each other. He preferred to direct money to where he could keep an eye on its owners. Fines and unprecedented new taxes impoverished the better-off, with knock-on effects on their tenants. Whether this was a calculated policy to reduce the north's strength or not, it certainly appeared so to some people; no one in Yorkshire could believe in the 'evil councillor' theory any longer. A serious, carefully planned uprising in Wakefield, thwarted by a last-minute betrayal, was intended, not just to change his advisors, but to remove the king himself. Although the uprising was stopped and its planners punished, Henry realised that something more than violence was needed to show these rebellious Yorkshire folk who was master, and so, in 1541, he set out on a Royal Progress to the north, with the intention of demonstrating his power.

Royal progresses were miracles of organisation and provided a huge, if temporary, boost to the local economy of the places visited. They were opportunities for a king to distribute royal largesse, hear local complaints and receive homage from local dignitaries. Henry knew how to employ both carrot and stick. The emphasis of the Progress was to be on the King's gracious forgiveness for past rebellions. Henry wanted submission above all. The chief men of towns involved in the Pilgrimage of Grace (like Hull and York) had to take part in a carefully staged public drama, meeting the king on their knees, offering grovelling requests for his clemency and publicly swearing allegiance to him. They also, wisely, offered gifts of money.

Henry took with him 4,000 soldiers just in case (and avoided Wakefield and the West Riding), but, wishing to impress York, also made grand arrangements at King's Manor (the recently acquired residence of the ex-Abbot of St Mary's Abbey) where he hoped to meet the King of Scotland for talks (James was his brother-in-law, but far too close to the French for comfort).

James never came, but the Manor, beautified for the king, provided Catherine Howard, his young fifth wife, with opportunities to continue cuckolding him in comfort.

YORKSHIRE FOLK:
John Fisher: Bishop and Catholic martyr. Born in Beverley, Fisher rose to become the highly respected Bishop of Rochester. However, he refused to side with the king over his divorce from Catherine of Aragon, something Henry never forgave. Fisher also opposed Henry's assumption of the position as head of the Church. When the king introduced an Oath of Succession, which forced the swearer to acknowledge the children of Henry and Anne as legitimate heirs to the throne, under pain of being guilty of treason, Fisher refused to take it and, having been tricked into saying that Henry was not the real head of the Church, was tried for treason and sentenced to be hanged, drawn and quartered. Public outcry made the king change this to beheading.

PLACES TO VISIT:
The Old Grammar School: Hull
The Great Tythe Barn: Bolton Abbey
Ryedale Folk Museum: Hutton le Hole, North York Moors

12

ELIZABETHAN AND JACOBEAN YORKSHIRE

There be not in all this country [county] ten gentlemen that do favour and allow of Her Majesty's proceedings in the course of religion.

Sir Ralph Sadler

Catholicism did not die quietly in Yorkshire, particularly in Dales villages which concealed many who refused to give up their faith. Nearly all the leading families in Nidderdale, and half of those in Richmondshire, were Catholic, which probably explains why no one in Yorkshire seems to have suffered under Henry VIII's Catholic daughter, Mary. However, things changed when Elizabeth I took the throne. Recusancy laws, fining those who refused to go to one of the new Protestant church services every Sunday, were enacted, though their enforcement depended on the religious zeal of local magistrates. Severe penalties for harbouring priests were also imposed, and for priests themselves, death.

THE RISING OF THE NORTH

The north-south divide in Britain had existed since Viking times, but the north had always been, if not the financial equal of the south, at least important militarily because of the power of its lords and the toughness of its people. That ancient importance was draining away as the Tudor monarchs, always fearing rebellion and advised by politically astute ministers, centralised government in London.

The old northern aristocratic families, the Percys, Nevilles and Cliffords, deeply resented this, coming as it did on top of the unwelcome religious changes. In 1569, the eleventh year of Elizabeth's reign, they rebelled, intending to replace the queen with her Catholic cousin, Mary, Queen of Scots, whom she was holding prisoner.

The Rising was led by Charles Neville, Earl of Westmorland, and Thomas Percy, Earl of Northumberland (their old family enmity forgotten). As so often happened in rebellions, news of it got out before all its planned elements were in place, and so its leaders had to act prematurely. They moved speedily to occupy Durham, where Mass was celebrated in the cathedral. Ladies Westmorland and Northumberland were present at this event, enthusiastically tearing up the new Reformed prayer books, and so was one Richard Norton (of Norton Conyers), wearing a huge gold crucifix around his neck and carrying an old Pilgrimage of Grace banner.

The plan was to then move south, capture York and free Mary (who knew about the plot) from Tutbury, where she was being held. The rebels hoped for help from France, a Catholic country, where Mary had briefly been queen consort.

Unfortunately for the conspirators their hopes for a mass uprising of English Catholics were too optimistic (this was also the case with the Gunpowder Plotters thirty-six years later). Ordinary people did not rise against their rulers lightly – especially if they doubted the outcome – and, as we shall see, their caution was justified. Seeing that they did not have enough men to capture York, as had been the plan, the rebel army turned aside and besieged Sir George Bowes (ancestor of the museum founder) at Barnard Castle. When he capitulated eleven days later, they marched south, still hoping in vain for a popular uprising of faithful Catholics. It never came, and hearing that the Earl of Essex had raised an army against them the troops began to melt away.

The leaders' nerve broke and they ran, Northumberland to Scotland (where he was eventually handed over to Elizabeth by the Earl of Morton, an old enemy of Mary's), and Westmorland to Flanders, where, given a small pension by the King of Spain, he died in poverty.

Thus ended the Rising of the North, the last open attempt to return England to Catholicism. It brought disaster not just on its leaders but on ordinary Catholics as well because Elizabeth, with the true Tudor fury, took violent revenge. Northumberland's beheading was inevitable, but the lands of every important person involved were also seized and Elizabeth demanded that at least 700 people be executed in North Yorkshire, particularly in the Catholic Dales. Local officers seem to have dragged their feet over this, but even so about 450 people 'wholly of the meanest sort of people', according to a contemporary source, were hanged. In York captured Catholic priests were hanged, drawn and quartered, and a new Act of Parliament passed, making this the punishment of anyone found harbouring one. Margaret Clitheroe, York's most famous Catholic martyr, was to become a victim of this law. An ordinary woman, wife to a butcher in the Shambles, she was converted to Catholicism shortly after the Rising and was arrested in 1586 for helping priests. When she refused to plead either innocent or guilty to the charge she was pressed to death at the toll booth prison on Ouse Bridge. It was very unusual for a woman – or indeed anyone – to be executed in this horrible way, but there were good reasons why Margaret chose not to plead. Her family, including her husband, were important people in the city (though not Catholics themselves).

Refusal to plead meant that a trial could not be held and so no evidence which might have implicated them could be revealed. In addition, the lack of a conviction meant that her family could not have their property seized, as was the penalty for the family of criminals.

Elizabeth, on hearing the news of this execution, declared herself horrified.

The north was finally cowed; the Nevilles and other Yorkshire gentry were deprived of their lands, and although the Percys eventually recovered their title, they were forbidden to live in the north. (Southerners picked up the confiscated properties.)

Time was also running out for Mary, Queen of Scots, now firmly established as Elizabeth's chief danger. In the aftermath of the rebellion she was moved by her unsympathetic keeper, George, Earl of Shrewsbury (husband of the redoubtable Bess of Hardwick), from place to place, including Tutbury, Wingfield Manor and Chatsworth House, as well as a converted hunting lodge in Sheffield (which locals will tell you she still haunts).

RECOVERY AND GROWTH

If you weren't a Catholic, things became rather better for you from the middle of the sixteenth century. Trade improved, markets expanded and ordinary people thrived as the new industries and improved farming methods enabled them to earn more money. The population rose considerably (to about five million by 1640). Famine was still a threat, however, and diseases of various sorts, including our old friend the Plague, flared up from time to time.

York benefitted from the general revival of trade in Europe, with flourishing markets on Tuesday, Thursday and Saturday, and a new cloth market in the Common Hall (the Guildhall). The city's freemen mostly lived within the walls, but an increasing class of professionals, such as lawyers,

preferred to live outside the corporation's jurisdiction around the Minster, the castle and King's Manor.

Other Yorkshire towns were doing better, too. Howden fair (famous later for horses) expanded and attracted merchants from London, while George, the Earl of Shrewsbury (Mary's erstwhile guardian) began to exploit the minerals such as lead and coal on his large estate at Bawtry, bringing trade from all over Europe. The money from it flowed into the ever-swelling pockets of the Earl and his family.

In Sheffield the metal-workers were capturing the cheap end of the cutlery market; Doncaster prospered and in Pontefract liquorice-growing (encouraged by the ubiquitous Earl, who had estates there) was successfully introduced.

By the time of James I, Leeds' population had doubled to 6,000. It was the West Riding's chief cloth market, specialising in expert finishing of broadcloth. One of its merchants, John Harrison, was rich enough to build St John's church, a grammar school, an almshouse and a street of buildings.

As for Halifax, 'There is nothing so admirable in this town,' said William Camden, the great Elizabethan antiquary, 'as the industry of the inhabitants, who, notwithstanding an unprofitable soil not fit to live in, have so flourished by the cloth trade (which within these last seventy years they fell to) that they are both very rich and have gained a great reputation for it ...'

The success of the cloth industry was only part of the reason for West Yorkshire's success. Lack of tight manorial control in areas such as the less fertile western areas meant that smallholders there, needing additional income to support their families, were free to develop supplementary skills such as weaving, metal-working, coal-mining, tanning, leather-working and charcoal burning, all of which could be combined with farming. Such places welcomed innovators and immigrants bringing new skills and techniques.

Leather-working became an important, if smelly, industry in the area. Thousands of hides were brought from London by water. Tanneries – huge soaking pits where the hides were tanned by means of oak bark – were sited, for obvious reasons, on the outside of towns. (It was said that tanners had to marry tanner lasses because no one else could stand the smell!)

In the Dales, the government encouraged home industries such as the production of knitted stockings, worn by both sexes and gartered above the knee with woven garters. One of the centres of the hosiery trade was in Richmond, where wool was provided for home knitters who sold the finished pairs back. The target was three dozen pairs a week, so everyone in the family had to be involved. With population growth and the ancient custom of dividing land equally between sons, farms had become very small, sometimes just a few acres. Knitting soon became an essential part of the local economy. In Dent, famous for its male and female knitters, they eventually developed a way of knitting with one hand, using wooden knitting sheaths (which could be stuck in the belt) holding one of the needles. Multitasking is not a modern invention.

In Yorkshire as a whole most people still earned their living purely through agriculture, However, times were slowly changing as enclosure became more acceptable. In Holderness most towns still had two huge common fields that stretched for hundreds of acres, but in some places farmers were agreeing to divide them up or turn them into grassland. While drainage schemes had improved some boggy land, allowing thriving wheat and cattle production, the technology of drainage was in its infancy. Areas like the valley of the Hull were regularly flooded, producing occasional clouds of malaria-bearing mosquitoes (malaria was endemic in many parts of England). The low-lying townships in the eastern and southern parts of the Vale of York were also badly drained; great for pasture and wildlife but no good for crops. In some places efficient drainage wasn't achieved until the invention of steam engines.

In the lower part of the Wolds, as in Holderness, many huge common fields remained, and some of the characteristic dry valleys had lynchets (terraces) to extend the arable. Occasional attempts were made to plough the thin soil of the High Wolds, but sheep and rabbit warrens were more common in the uplands. Deserted village sites like Warram Percy became vast sheep runs.

Common fields had more or less completely disappeared in the Dales by the end of Elizabeth's reign; meadow and pasture were now divided into small closes. Grazing rights on the high moors were essential to the Dales' way of life; sheep grazed there in the summer, while cattle occupied the lower pastures. In winter the cattle were brought down into the closes and fed on hay, while the sheep were driven down from the tops to take their place in the lower pastures.

Lead-mining in the area was still a fairly small-scale industry, but in the early seventeenth century John Sayer of Great Worsall sank and drained the Marrick mines in Swaledale. Soon, high above the road from Pately Bridge to Grassington, the lead workers employed by Sir Stephen Proctor of Fountains Abbey lived and worked on

Greenhow Hill and spoil heaps and smelt mills began to become a feature of the countryside.

Fishing continued to be very important in the sixteenth and seventeenth centuries, employing a huge number of people all around the Yorkshire coast. However, at the end of the sixteenth century Whitby grew considerably as a port as a result of the alum trade. At the time alum, an expensive chemical, was important for medicine, in curing leather and for fixing dyed cloths. The Papal States of the time held a monopoly on both production and sale, but in the reign of James I Thomas Chaloner, owner of an estate at Guisborough, noticed while on a visit to Italy that the rock being processed there for alum was similar to that on his own land. Chaloner secretly brought workmen to develop the industry in Yorkshire, and alum began to be produced near Sandsend Ness, three miles (5km) from Whitby. As the home industry began to flourish, the government banned foreign imports of alum. The sharp-eyed Mr Chaloner was soon in happy possession of huge fortune.

The government, keen to reduce imports, encouraged ideas from abroad. Charcoal blast furnaces, an improvement on the old iron bloomeries, were introduced from Lorraine and built by the Earl of Shaftesbury at Kimberworth and Wadsley in South Yorkshire, where they served nearby forges worked by French immigrants on the Don at Allcliffe. Steel, a mixture of iron and carbon, essential for making the sharp edges of knives, had been imported from the Continent but now steelworks sprang up around Rotherham and Sheffield to serve the cutlery industry. (The demand for underwood to make charcoal for such industries rocketed.)

For domestic fires, coal, as well as turf (peat, not grass), was increasingly used rather than wood. Coal mines in West Yorkshire, still small local businesses, supplied some, but most was still sent in barges from Newcastle.

By 1555 the state of the roads and the slowness and cost of transport had become a matter of national importance and so a system of maintenance was devised making each parish responsible for its roads. Every able-bodied house-holder had to spend four (later six) days a year working on local roads. By the end of the sixteenth century enterprising people such as those in Doncaster Corporation had set up postal services to important places like London along the improved roads, and carriers were (very slowly, in ox carts) carting supplies and parcels to most towns in England, stopping at the newly opened inns and alehouses which had proliferated. By 1577 Yorkshire JPs were struggling to impose licensing schemes on the county's 239 inns and the 3,700 alehouses. They did not entirely succeed.

HOUSING

Some of the most interesting and beautiful houses in Yorkshire were built during the sixteenth and seventeenth centuries as the county grew wealthier. The demonstration of one's wealth was as important as ever, and in times of peace even more important than defence. Members of the prestigious Council of the North were among those rich and ambitious enough to compete in architectural display. King's Manor in York, home of the Council, was enlarged by its Jacobean president, Sir Thomas Wentworth, Earl of Strafford, and Sir Thomas Eynns, its secretary, built Heslington Hall in expensive brick. Though some of the new houses, such as Snape Castle, harked back to the past with towers and crenellations, their military usefulness was minimal.

Glass was expensive and therefore essential to making a grand impression. It could only be made in relatively small sizes so the large 'lights' that were becoming popular required stone mullions (vertical struts) and transoms (hori-zontal struts) to support the leaded glazing. Nearly all the great Elizabethan and Jacobean houses of Yorkshire – Burton Agnes, Gilling Castle, Burton Constable Hall, Howsham Hall – have expensive and showy ranges of such windows.

Burton Agnes Hall was designed by Robert Smythson (an early member of the evolving profession of architects) for another member of the Council of the North, Sir Henry Griffith. Although traditional in many ways, it has the latest novelty of a long gallery, intended to display the paintings and exotic treasures of its owner as well as a beautifully carved oak staircase supported by a massive newel post (unusual at the time).

No one could compete with the wealth of Bess of Hardwick and her husband the Earl of Shrewsbury when it came to improving houses (of which they had many, scattered throughout their estates in the Midlands and south-west Yorkshire), but lesser mortals could at least add a new shell to their timber-framed houses or a fashionable entrance with columns and carvings. They could also enhance the interior and improve heat retention with wainscoting (wood panelling) and new fireplaces.

In the Halifax district wealthy clothiers and local gentry produced their own unique smaller versions of aristocratic houses, an attractive mixture of Renaissance and Gothic details.

The houses of the less wealthy were improving too, with proper chimneys and a greater range of furniture and household goods, but those of the poorest folks, perhaps inevitably, remained pretty much as primitive as before.

THE POOR

The problem of what to do with the poor, greater after the Dissolution of the Monasteries, led to the enactment of Poor Laws, first under Henry VIII and then under Elizabeth I, whose Act of 1601 remained in force until the nineteenth century. One of the contributory factors to poverty was inflation, which began to increase during the sixteenth century. It was low by our standards, but disastrous in a time when wages were slow to rise and it particularly hit areas where common grazing had disappeared.

Ninety per cent of the population were still living in the countryside. Inflation and static wages meant that they were forced to rely more and more on their own little plot of land and their animals to supplement their income. The poor often had to scrape a living from many different sources; being able to graze a milch cow or a few sheep on common land was essential for many. When commons were enclosed many small free resources also disappeared: bracken for bedding, holly and other foliage for winter feed, flowers that could be bunched and sold in the market, wild food like berries, gorse for fuel and fencing. Landowners laying greedy hands on common pasture to extend their lands sometimes found themselves facing the scythes and pitchforks of village rebellion and though some were successfully taken to court, in the long run, then as now, those with more money were bound to win.

Under the new Poor Law legislation, originally intended to provide care for those who could not work, 'Overseers of the Poor' were to be elected in each parish to draw up a list of the impoverished in their area and levy a Poor Rate on property owners for their upkeep. The poor were divided into 'deserving' and 'undeserving'. The former were those who wanted to find work but either couldn't, or were unable, to work; the latter were vagrants, beggars, etc. who, according to public opinion, did not want to work. The 'deserving' poor who could work were to be employed in some useful way for wages; those who could not work were to be placed in almshouses or given outdoor relief (food or money); the 'undeserving' poor were to be whipped or branded and returned to their own birth parish if found wandering. Children of the poor were to be apprenticed to some useful trade. Later, Houses of Correction (often known as Bridewells) were established to house petty offenders given short sentences. About two-thirds of the inmates were women assumed or proved to be prostitutes.

These poor laws were well-intentioned, but there was no oversight of how they were administered, and their interpretation varied widely in different parishes. The dreaded workhouse, however, was still in the future.

YORKSHIRE FOLK:

Mary Ward: Born in Mulwith, North Yorkshire, Mary became a Catholic nun in Saint-Omer. She decided not to shut herself away in a nunnery but dedicate herself to an active ministry. At the age of 24 she found herself surrounded by a band of devoted companions determined to work under her guidance. In 1609 they established themselves as a religious community at Saint-Omer and opened schools for girls, something that was very controversial at the time. The two organisations she founded, the Congregation of Jesus and the Institute of the Blessed Virgin Mary, still provide schools around the world.

PLACES TO VISIT:

Burton Agnes Hall: Burton Agnes, East Yorkshire
The Shambles, York: Half-timbered houses built out over the street
Temple Newsom House: Leeds

13

THE CIVIL WARS

The old antagonisms of religion did not disappear with increased prosperity. Elizabeth I had managed, by a deliberate inexactitude of language in the 1559 Religious Settlement Act to keep the different religious groups in order. She declared that none of her subjects should be questioned about their beliefs or practices 'as long as they shall in their outward conversation show themselves quiet and not manifestly repugnant to the laws of the realm'. The unquiet and repugnant were punished severely.

England was now a Protestant country, but there were many types of Protestant, interpreting the Bible in their own way and, being human, all believing themselves to be right. Some, mostly followers of a French theologian, John Calvin, held that churches should be solely for preaching; no robes, statues, ceremonies, or altars should have a place in the Church of England. Often called Puritans, they grew in power and numbers as Elizabeth's reign drew to its close.

People in the more independently minded towns of Yorkshire, particularly those in the West Riding, were drawn to the simplicity of Puritanism and its dislike of display and Church hierarchy. Some even went so far as to believe that they should cut themselves off, not just from the Church of England but from their own degenerate country: at least two, William Bradfield of Austerfield and his wife, sailed on the *Mayflower* to help found a colony in America.

In 1632 Archbishop Richard Neile began to remove Puritan vicars from the diocese of York, but by then some of Yorkshire's ancient gentry were leaning towards Puritanism. Meanwhile its influence had spread among MPs in Parliament, and those who might once have supported the status quo were beginning to feel enough confidence in their own judgement to criticise the way in which the country was governed. The king, Charles I, made matters worse. He was a man with little understanding of or sympathy with ordinary people. He had been brought up to believe in the Divine Right of Kings and appreciated neither compromise nor Parliament's attempts to control his spending. His high-handed dealings with the House of Commons alienated members, both Puritan and Anglican (Church of England).

It would be a mistake to imagine that those who were to became supporters of Parliament during the Civil War were all steeple-hatted haters of dancing and Christmas, or that those who favoured the king's party were plumed revellers; town-dwelling businessmen tended to side with Parliament while the more conservative country people tended to support the king, but the arguments on both sides attracted and divided all sorts of families, whatever headgear they might favour.

Conflict seemed unavoidable, and yet, in Yorkshire, as the two parties developed, there was a strong publicly expressed desire, even in its more Puritan areas, not to get involved. For many people, arguments about government were irrelevant to their own lives; they preferred to keep their heads down, remaining neutral. Unfortunately, this was not an option either side would agree to.

Charles had already (in 1642) decided that York, the second city in the country, was a better place for the court than London and established himself there. On 22 August he raised his standard in Nottingham, declaring war.

What followed was, for Yorkshire, several years of all the miseries of civil war. Buildings were destroyed, trade halted, churches vandalised. Troops of both sides were billeted on ordinary people who were then subjected to all the usual unruliness and thievery of common soldiers. Few accounts tell of the sufferings of ordinary folk during this time, folk whose horses, food, fodder and even beds might be requisitioned. There is no record of how many civilians died, but there were inevitably arbitrary shootings and many rapes. Officers sometimes had little control over men ill-paid and supplied, who often had to 'live off the land', which, in fact, meant living off the land's owners. In the North Riding, Scottish troops, allies of Parliament, terrorised the people as in the old days. Hull, York, Skipton, Bradford and Pontefract endured long sieges and Scarborough Castle changed hands seven times, as well as being besieged twice.

Charles' first concern was getting supplies of arms, but Parliament controlled London, with its massive store of armaments at the Tower, so the king marched quickly towards Hull, intending to get possession of its arsenal. Parliament, however, moved even faster, sending a message to the Governor of Hull, Sir John Hotham, to refuse the king entrance to the city. When Charles and his commander in the north, William Cavendish, the Earl of Newcastle (a grandson of Bess of Hardwick) arrived it was to find the gates locked and the walls manned. A subsequent siege failed: Hull was too well provisioned. Charles and his troops withdrew to York to gather more supporters. (Later in the war Hotham became disillusioned with the Parliamentary leadership and plotted to surrender the town. He was stopped in time and, having betrayed both sides, was executed.)

The Parliamentary forces in Yorkshire were led by the wonderfully named Ferdinando, Lord Fairfax, and his son

Sir Thomas. They began their campaign by marching into the West Riding, where they were sure of support, and at first won a number of minor victories. Newcastle (now a Marquis) followed them and, considerably outnumbered, they were narrowly defeated at Adwalton Moor. This was a devastating blow for Parliament, which now only held Hull in Yorkshire.

Fortunately for the Parliamentarians it was at this point that their Scottish allies, who had religious objections to the way in which certain practices of the Church of England had been forced on them, invaded the north. Newcastle, who had been mopping up Parliamentary forces in Yorkshire, was forced to go north to deal with the Scots, allowing Lord Fairfax's brother-in-law, Sir William Constable, to lead his forces out of Hull, where they had been trapped, to achieve a victory in the Wolds and capture both Bridlington and Whitby.

In Newcastle's absence, Royalist troops commanded by Colonel John Bellasys continued the Royalist campaign, but were repulsed twice at Bradford. In 1644, Sir Thomas Fairfax defeated Bellasys' force decisively at Selby. Newcastle, returning hastily to York to support him, found himself besieged in York Castle by a joint force of Scots and Parliamentarians.

The fortunes of war were now turning in Parliament's favour, but news came that the king's nephew, the young and dashing Prince Rupert, was advancing from the west to lift the siege, gathering troops as he came.

Most of the fighting in the Civil War took place not in great set piece battles, but rather in squalid ambushes from behind hedges in narrow lanes. However, the encounter between

Rupert and Newcastle and the combined Parliamentary and Scots armies, including a well-organised cavalry wing under Oliver Cromwell, resulted in one of the most decisive battles ever fought in Yorkshire, and probably the biggest in terms of numbers ever fought on English soil (as decisive as Towton, though less bloody). On 2 July 1644, at Marston Moor, Rupert's horse were defeated (and his beloved dog, Boye, killed). Newcastle's infantry were destroyed. 'God made them stubble to our swords,' said Cromwell.

Subsequently the remaining Royalist garrisons in the north fell, one after another, and most of the old castles they defended were 'slighted' or dismantled so that they could not be re-fortified; Pontefract and Sheffield Castles were razed to the ground. Royalist power in the north had been destroyed. Prince Rupert retreated to Chester with the remains of the army and the poor Marquis of Newcastle, unwilling 'to endure the laughter of the court', abandoned the king's cause and fled to the Netherlands immediately after Marston Moor.

The Civil Wars continued intermittently until 1651. Eventually, the king himself, through his own devious obstinacy and inept but unforgiveable attempts at secret deals with foreign powers, was led, step by step, to his own trial and execution. Most members of Parliament were uncomfortable with killing a king but had given up trying to deal with him; however, fifteen Yorkshiremen were among the judges at Charles' trial and six were present at his execution, the ideal of neutrality long forgotten.

YORKSHIRE FOLK:

Andrew Marvell, Parliamentarian poet and MP. Born in Winestead-in-Holderness, near Hull, he was elected MP for Hull in 1659 during Cromwell's Protectorate, but is much more famous for his poetry including 'On Appleton House' and 'To His Coy Mistress', which has the lines:

'The grave's a fine and private place
But none, I think, do there embrace ...'

PLACES TO VISIT:
Shibden Hall: near Halifax
Arksey village: sixteenth- and seventeenth-century almshouses, church and old school
Beggar's Bridge: Glaisedale, North Yorkshire. Pack Horse bridge dated 1619 (with a romantic story attached)
Marston Moor Battlefield and monument: Long Marston, North Yorkshire

14

YEARS OF EXPANSION, 1680–1780

TOWNS

During the late seventeenth century the slow migration of people from the countryside to the town began to gather speed. Identity was still very much bound up with locality, however: a fisherman from Scarborough did not have much in common with a Dales farmer or West Riding weaver. People might move to the market town of their 'country', but seldom further afield. Being a Yorkshire man or woman didn't mean a lot yet.

Outsiders' interest in Yorkshire was growing, though, as the new monarchy of Charles II produced a flourishing of artistic and scientific curiosity. Travellers such as Cecily Fiennes and Daniel Defoe ventured into the barbarian north and wrote about their experiences, while others, perhaps inspired by *Dr Johnson's Dictionary*, exclaimed over the strange words in the dialects of North and East Yorkshire.

The West Riding was the main beneficiary of the new mobility of workers. Its better economic opportunities attracted ambitious young people from villages and farms

in the whole surrounding area. By 1672, half of the county's
350,000 people lived in the West Riding. After 1700 population growth in all towns increased considerably, possibly due
to access to better food, earlier marriage and a wider choice of
mates, though early death rates remained high.

York was still the most important city in the north, but it
was beginning to lose its manufacturing eminence to Leeds
and Sheffield. Daniel Defoe thought that 'no other city in
England is better furnished with provisions of every kind,
nor any so cheap'. Town houses for county families such
as the Bourchiers of Beningborough Hall were built along
Micklegate and the Earl of Burlington designed the beautiful assembly rooms as a gathering place for the glittering
parties who attended the races on the Knavesmire. Rather
less glittering parties attended the hangings there, including
that of Dick Turpin.

Other towns benefitted from the general peace and pros-
perity. Beverley acquired its fine market cross in 1714; Ripon
and Howden became famous for their horse fairs; Bedale,
Stokesley, Yarm and other towns were rebuilt in brick; and
Wakefield's cramped streets were replaced with a graceful
Georgian square around the new St John's church.

Cloth production remained the most important industry in the county. The West Riding, like the cutlers of Hallamshire, concentrated on the cheap end of the textile market. Its special characteristic was the independent nature of its family units, which combined cloth-production with farming. This made the area particularly flexible compared with the rest of the county: it required little capital to set up a loom and there were few large-scale masters controlling prices. Leeds, where capitalism was on the rise, was the exception: there the big worsted manufacturers were much more powerful, able to employ hundreds of out-workers on piece work.

Markets were still held outside until wealthy clothiers, no doubt fed up with standing in the Yorkshire rain, began to club together to build cloth halls in which to display and sell their goods. Halifax was the first to have a Piece Hall – a piece is a length of cloth – in 1708. (It was replaced in 1779 by the present much grander one.) Rival towns hastened to get their cloth under cover: Wakefield in 1710, Leeds in 1711 and Huddersfield (where the unfortunate sellers of the coarse cloths called kerseys had previously been forced to display them hanging over the church wall) in 1766.

In 1699 Parliament passed a bill making it possible for the rivers Aire and Calder to be made navigable to Leeds. Locks and cuts joined Knottingley to Leeds by 1704 and two years later the river Calder was made navigable between Castleford and Wakefield. In 1721 the navigation was extended to Selby. These improvements to its accessibility gave Leeds such a boost that it now quickly surpassed its rivals, and by the end of the eighteenth century was the largest and most important manufacturing town in Yorkshire. Soon new industries such as pottery, chemicals, soap-boiling and sugar refining filled the Leeds air with fumes not always beneficial to the inhabitants.

Sheffield's rise continued. Its cutlery industry had been helped considerably by the genteel fashion for forks, which, although reputedly invented by a Byzantine princess hundreds of years before, had hitherto been considered a foreign fad by British people. Cutlery manufacture was still largely carried out at home in a cutler's smithy at the rear of the house. Sheffield plate was invented at about the same time, making a cheaper version of silver cutlery available to more people. It quickly became popular and platers grew rich.

Nail-making was a common secondary employment for farmers near the cutlery district. The centre of the nailing industry was the Black Country, but Yorkshire came a close second, using iron from the Tankersley seam, smelted by a group of gentry iron-masters. Slitting-mills, which handled the difficult task of splitting bars of iron into thin flat lengths, were introduced in the seventeenth century and travelling chapmen supplied the nailers from them. Nailing was a useful seasonal trade, helped by huge exports to the American colonies. Though originally a purely domestic business carried out, like cutlery-making, in sheds at the back of people's houses, nailers-turned-middlemen, such as Samuel and Aaron Walker, could acquire enough capital to start their own iron and steelworks.

In 1742 Benjamin Huntsman moved to Handsworth and began to experiment with making steel in crucibles. At first the local cutlers refused to use his harder steel, but competition with French cutlers eventually forced them to accept it. Huntsman kept his methods secret until, according to legend, a starving beggar, given shelter by the fire in the works, stole the secret. So began the great Sheffield crucible steel industry.

Coal was still a small-scale industry, lucrative but limited by the cost of transport. The potential power of steam was already understood and employed in Newcomen engines used to pump water from pits, but steam trains were still in the future. Horse-drawn trucks on wooden railways carried coal from the mines on the Rockingham estate at Greasborough.

FORNACE DA VETRI.

English glass-making had been encouraged by Parliament and well-established in areas such as Rosedale, where wood for the charcoal that fired the furnaces, built by immigrants from Lorraine, could be easily obtained. However, by the late sixteenth century the wholesale deforestation of the country was beginning to worry the government and it banned the use of wood in furnaces. Glassworks changed to coal and moved to coal-producing areas such as Silkstone, near Barnsley, Bolderstone and Catcliffe. The Lorrainers' sophisticated techniques produced fine crystal and window glass as well as the cheap green glass used in bottles.

Potteries, once small local businesses, grasped the opportunities to expand provided by improved waterways. Leeds Old Pottery was the first large-scale enterprise of this kind. It produced the cream pottery known as Leedsware in many different designs, including perforated and basketwork.

Hull, the county's fourth largest port, was becoming very congested within its city walls. A series of Improvement Acts dealt with some of the problems, but it was not until 1774 that the old brick city walls were removed to allow construction of three huge new docks. Hull men had fished as far afield as Greenland for years but it was only in the 1730s that a small fleet of ships ventured north to catch whales, the oil of which was used for lamps. Blubber houses were built in both Hull and Whitby, but the industry remained small until the nineteenth century.

Peace and plenty brought an interest in 'polite' living and civic pride. Towns competed, with public buildings, theatres, concert halls, assembly rooms and paved streets lit with oil lamps. Fashionable new town houses housed a better educated middle class with a taste for newspapers such as the *Leeds Mercury*. Local men such as Thomas Gent and Francis Drake (not the explorer) wrote books celebrating the history and topography of their towns, one of which, Scarborough, was to become almost the equal of Bath as a resort of the wealthy in search of health and entertainment, thanks to its medicinal waters.

The discovery of sulphur and chalybeate springs in the seventeenth century led to the development of a new type of town in Yorkshire where people could come to 'take the cure'. What needed to be cured varied, and was often merely boredom, but the daily morning immersion in (or draught of) mineral water preceded an afternoon and evening of mild exercise, socialising, dancing, flirting, and serious gambling which appealed to the wealthy, not just of Yorkshire but of other parts of the country including Scotland. Indeed, some people regarded Scarborough as not just equal but *superior* to Bath, all the more because taking the waters there could be combined with the new fashion of sea-bathing. As swimwear had not yet been invented everyone swam naked, but bathing machines (a sort of enclosed carriage) were invented in mid-century for the accommodation of embarrassed females and the elderly. Other healing waters produced rival spas at Harrogate, Boston Spa, Tadcaster and the remote White Wells near Ilkley.

IMPROVED TRANSPORT

Increases in manufacturing put even more pressure on the need for better methods of transporting goods. Rivers were still the best way and soon the new navigations of the Aire and Calder were joined by improvements to other river systems.

The Ouse was still a vital waterway for barges carrying cloth, lead, butter, corn, rapeseed, tallow and other products down to the Humber. The goods that they brought back from other parts of England supplied a wide area around York. The Ouse was still tidal in those days, which delayed shipping during low tide. In 1757 a lock, dam and weir were constructed at Naburn to prevent the water falling too far. (A small banqueting Hall added later to facilitate the wealthy Trustees' annual feast is still there.)

The Don was also tidal as far as Wilsick House, but it too was improved until by 1751 it was navigable all the way to Tinsley.

An ambitious plan to connect the cloth towns of the West Riding with those in Lancashire and ultimately to the port of Liverpool seemed at first too costly, involving as it did the crossing of the Pennines, but bit by bit, as money was subscribed, the Leeds–Liverpool Canal was achieved, though not fully completed until 1816. The first navvies, as its builders came to be known (from 'navigation') were mainly farm labourers (Irish navvies came later with the building of the railways). The work was hard and dangerous and a number of people died, especially in the construction of Gannow and Foulridge Tunnels.

The Tudor system of making parishes maintain their own roads had worked well enough when traffic was infrequent, but the highways connecting towns deteriorated disastrously in the years after the Civil War. This was partly due to increased road carriage and partly to the advent of stagecoaches, which now ran between most of the big towns and cut up the roads terribly. One could get a stagecoach

to London from the Black Swan in Coney Street in York '(if God permits) every Thursday at five in the morning'.

A series of Acts set up private trusts (rather like PFIs) which were to improve the highways in return for tolls. Toll gates (or turnpikes, from a type of barrier) were set up and a scale of charges for road users displayed on a board. Although these trusts were supposed to be time limited, they were lucrative and so a reason could always be found for renewing them. The first one in Yorkshire was on the Rochdale to Halifax road, financed, as were others, by local merchants, 'for the benefit of trade'. The new turnpikes, though inspiring some to violence at having to pay for what had been free, were a success. In 1754 the journey from London to Manchester took four and a half days, but thirty years later it took just over a day.

In hilly areas devoid of rivers or turnpikes pack horses remained the best method of transport. Strings of packhorses, sometimes as long as forty, carried goods from country farm to market in the towns, particularly in the West Riding. Improvements, some of them still visible, to these trails were made throughout the seventeenth and eighteenth centuries. They include the famous stone packhorse bridges, which replaced wooden ones, 'causeys' (from 'causeways'), which were paths of large stone blocks over boggy ground, and guide stoops, usually found on moors, which were upright stones with information about destination and mileage carved on them – sometimes with a helpful hand pointing the way.

FARMING

Farming was changing: by the seventeenth century there were sixty market towns in Yorkshire. Farmers could now buy whatever they needed locally so that they were able to change to growing whatever best suited their land. They had, however, to pay their farm labourers more to stop them leaving the land for the better wages in industrial towns. (Things were very different down south where farm labourers' wages were at an all-time low.) New ideas were abroad, and although many farmers, by nature cautious, obstinately refused to alter their ways, others were keen to try them, even adopting a new improved plough, the Rotherham, based on Dutch models, which became popular in many parts of Yorkshire.

One of the most important innovations was the inclusion of turnips and clover in crop rotations; they were better than the traditional peas and replaced the need to leave the arable to lie fallow for a season. These new crops provided additional winter feed as well as fixing nitrogen in the soil, and allowed land to be used more intensely without damaging its productivity.

Other crops gaining popularity included potatoes, grown at first in family gardens. They were introduced to Holderness where they flourished in the rich soil, eventually becoming an important crop. Rape had been grown for centuries, mostly for oil or sheep fodder, but it began to be planted more frequently on suitable land such as low-lying areas of the Vale of York. Even hop growing was tried, with some success, in the Hatfield Chase area.

In the North Riding some farmers began to specialise in dairying, sending their excellent butter in firkins to London or to the coast for export abroad. In Swaledale, however, things went a different way as the demand for lead piping in towns grew. There, farmers who had previously done a little lead mining extended their activities and became lead miners who did a little farming.

This was the great age of Parliamentary enclosure of common land. Although some had already been enclosed either by powerful landlords or by tenants' agreement, much still remained. When agreement with tenants could not be reached landowners, inspired by ideas of land improvement and keen to get the most out of their estates, resorted to private Acts of Parliament. Between 1750 and 1850, 4,000 Acts enclosed about 6 million acres of land in England and Wales. Those with grazing rights on the once common land were theoretically compensated with small closes, but, without any proper analysis of how important those rights were to family survival, the compensation was often inadequate and the fencing of the new plots – demanded in the Acts – expensive. The Wolds were particularly affected by enclosures. What had been wild sheepwalks and rabbit warrens were converted to arable. The present appearance of the Wolds with its huge rectangular fields and isolated brick farmhouses (each protected against the north-east wind by its windbreak of trees) comes from this time.

HOUSES

The biggest change in the houses of ordinary people was the increased use of brick. Yorkshire is well provided with clay, the substance of which bricks are made, and once its manufacture was mastered no more timber-framed houses were built. (The first brick house in an area was sometimes called 'the Red House'.) By the middle of the eighteenth century most houses were brick, built in the vernacular (domestic) style of their area. Roofs were still mostly thatched, though in towns Dutch pantiles imported from the Low Countries through Yarm were often used instead. Yorkshire sliding sash windows came in during the 1680s, though the gentry preferred vertical sashes (as in Middlethorpe Hall, near York). Mullioned windows continued in stone-built houses.

The dwellings of the gentry underwent much greater changes in style as their inhabitants adopted the classically inspired designs of the new profession of architecture. The Restoration of Charles II brought a great outburst of building as great landowners favoured with court sinecures spent the fortunes they amassed on acquiring great estates or enhancing their family's name and reputation by rebuilding the family seat. Some of the finest noblemen's houses in Britain were built here in the seventeenth and eighteenth centuries. Charles II had had the good sense not to punish those who had fought against his father (except for the signatories to his death warrant) so few landowners lost their lands on his accession. The best Restoration houses are mostly to be found in the Vale of York: Bell Hall at Naburn, Middlethorpe Hall, Newby Hall, Nunmonkton Hall.

In 1688 Charles' brother, James, last of the Stuarts, who had succeeded him, was removed from the throne by the (almost) bloodless Glorious Revolution, which established the Dutch William of Orange in his place. William rewarded well those who had helped him. One of them, Sir Thomas Osbourne, was created Duke of Leeds. He engaged the designer of Chatsworth, William Talman, to design a fine new house at Kiveton Park. Talman was obviously a hot property: Charles Howard, the Earl of Carlisle, also tried to engage him to create a new house to be called Castle Howard. They fell out badly so Howard employed Nicholas Hawksmoor and Sir John Vanbrugh instead. Hawksmoor was the well-known architect of London churches after the Great Fire. Vanbrugh was a more surprising choice: he was a popular playwright better known for plays that (outrageously!) sided with women. Castle Howard, the astonishing result of this fortunate collaboration, with its obelisk, scenic carriage drive, Temple of the Four Winds, statues and terrace, attempted to bring to Yorkshire some of the Italian scenes met with on the Grand Tour. There was nothing else like it at the time.

Political and family rivalry produced two great houses at Wentworth Castle and Wentworth Woodhouse. The politics of the day was divided between the Tories (Royalist) and the Whigs (constitutional monarchist). One of the great Tory officers of state, Thomas Wentworth (Lord Raby), was so infuriated that his Whig cousins had inherited Wentworth Woodhouse instead of him that he bought a nearby estate at Stainborough, changed its name to Wentworth Castle, and rebuilt it in the latest style, with an extensive gallery to display his collection of paintings acquired on Continental tours. He added a mock castle in the grounds, no doubt to justify the name.

His Whig cousin, confusingly named Thomas Watson-Wentworth, had begun adding a Baroque range to his newly inherited house at Wentworth Woodhouse, but by the time it was built architectural fashion had changed. Refusing to be beaten by his cousin, Thomas changed the style and orientation of the house by building, in the more fashionable Palladian style, an extremely long new front (said to be the longest front in the country) on the east side. The changes were greatly approved by the Earl of Burlington, amateur architect and style guru. His own estate was at Londesborough, where he built a fine house, now sadly demolished, but he lived mostly in London consorting with other noble fans of Palladio, a sixteenth-century Venetian, whose influential designs were based on Greek and Roman originals. Bretton Hall and Nostell Priory were also designed by members of Burlington's circle.

The influence of Classical thought and design lay heavily on the wealthy of the eighteenth century: Newby Hall had its gallery of classical sculptures, Fountains Abbey acquired a Classical approach with a Moon Pool and a Temple of Piety; Thomas Duncombe added a terrace with temples above Rievaulx Abbey, somewhat unsuitable, but lovely on a spring morning.

Those who could afford it did not stop at just rebuilding their houses; they wanted to rebuild the landscape around them. Villages were so untidy and full of unsightly people. Burlington moved the one spoiling his view of the Wolds at Londesborough; the Sykes family, Leeds and Hull merchants originally, removed and rebuilt a whole village at Sledmere, and Edwin Lascelles altered the landscape completely at Harewood (pronounced Ha-wood) when he demolished the village and the old Gawthorpe Hall to build Harewood House. What the hapless villagers, relocated to a new village at the gates, thought is not recorded.

PUNISHMENTS

A hardening of attitude towards the poor and criminals, probably connected with the population increase, led to what is now known (though not at the time) as 'the Bloody Code' – an ever-increasing list of capital offences – 220 by 1815. The laws were very proscriptive: you could be hanged for stealing goods of a value above five shillings. Fortunately for the majority of people convicted under these laws, judges and lawyers, unwilling to execute women, young boys and people obviously driven to crime by hunger, bent over backwards to find that the value of goods stolen was below five shillings in such cases. Transportation was considered a merciful and convenient solution and 850 men and women were eventually sent to Australia from courts in Hull and the East Riding. Considering the law's strictness, hanging was actually not a very common event in York, only two or three a year, although apparently causing sufficiently annoying traffic jams on hanging days at the Walmgate Bar gibbet for it to be removed to the castle.

Horrible punishments, including the burning of women for coining (the last was burnt in 1786) remained on the statute book until the law was revised in the Judgement of Death Act 1823.

Incidentally, it is Oliver Cromwell that Halifax has to thank for removing the Halifax gibbet (where people were beheaded by a sort of guillotine) remembered in the prayer 'from Hull, Hell and Halifax, good Lord deliver me.'

YORKSHIRE FOLK:

Captain James Cook FRS (1728–79): One of Yorkshire's most famous sons, he was a self-taught British explorer, navigator, cartographer, and captain in the Royal Navy. Cook made three voyages to the Pacific Ocean as well as being responsible for making detailed maps of Newfoundland. Under sealed orders he made the first recorded European contact with the people of the eastern coastline of Australia and Hawaii. He also circumnavigated New Zealand. Cook was attacked and killed in 1779 during his third exploratory voyage in the Pacific. He left behind a great legacy of scientific and geographical knowledge.

PLACES TO VISIT:

Castle Howard: North Yorkshire

Wentworth Woodhouse: Wentworth near Rotherham, South Yorkshire (open to the public for booked tours)

York Assembly Rooms: This is currently an Ask Italian restaurant but is really worth seeing to get a glimpse of fashionable Georgian life. The De Grey Rooms nearby are also worth a visit

The Georgian Theatre: Victoria Road, Richmond, North Yorkshire. One of the oldest (and tiniest) theatres in England. Recently restored to its original glory

15

THE INDUSTRIAL REVOLUTION, 1780–1850

The end of the Georgian period and the beginning of Victoria's reign was the time of 'those dark satanic mills'. Dark they might be, but for William Blake, who wrote 'Jerusalem', the word 'satanic' also meant 'creative'. The mills brought dynamic change, whether for good or ill.

Events in the wider world could no longer be ignored by ordinary people. The French Revolution filled many middle- and upper-class people with fear and distrust of working people, and the Napoleonic Wars gave manufacturers an unparalleled opportunity for growth, while also increasing the cost of food. America, hitherto an important place to sell English – and particularly Yorkshire – goods, became independent, keen to develop its own manufactures.

The northern toughness so valued (and feared) in previous centuries was even more important during the Industrial Revolution. People refused to be ground down either by wealthy businessmen or by interfering parliaments, though they were often defeated by both. Support for contentious national issues, such as the Repeal of the Corn Laws or universal suffrage and the Chartist Movement was particularly strong in Yorkshire, and, despite the terrible cost to themselves, workers kept those who employed them on their toes with riots and strikes whenever they were pressed too hard.

TEXTILES

Textile manufacture was probably still the county's most important industry at the time, but the skilled clothiers who had prospered in the middle of the eighteenth century were to see some of their grandchildren reduced to poverty as machines left them deskilled and vulnerable. Others were able to grasp opportunities that lifted them beyond the dreams of their grandparents.

Power Looms
The first of these was built in 1785 by Edmund Cartwright. They could only be used for cotton weaving to begin with, but their design was improved by various engineers and by 1850 there were about 260,000 looms, able to weave all types of fabrics. Handloom weavers were slowly put out of business.

Cotton
Cotton is a difficult material to spin and weave as it requires being kept damp. Before the advent of weaving machines handloom cotton weavers had to work in damp cellars. Beautiful printed cotton cloth had been imported here from India since the late seventeenth century, but it was an expensive import and the British government, wanting to encourage the creation of a home cotton-weaving industry, banned it, while still allowing imports of 'gamgee', raw cotton wool. The East India Company also helped to destroy the once-great Mughal fabric industry by

investing in the introduction of cotton-spinning machinery to Lancashire. Yorkshire towns just over the border in Craven benefitted as cotton mills were also built at Skipton, Barnoldswick and Settle.

The Factory System

Also introduced from Lancashire, this system, initially only used for cotton-spinning, involved installing many machines in a large mill and employing cheap, less skilled workers, to operate them. 'Women's work' had always been under-valued and paid less than men's, making them the obvious choice as workers in factories, and the small hands of children as young as 5 were ideal for tying broken threads. A strict, intrusive system of surveillance was imposed to stop workers talking, stealing or wasting time. It was his observations of this cruelty in cotton mills that led one of the founders of socialism in Britain, Robert Owen, to try his experiments in running a mill in New Lanark in Scotland on philanthropic principles.

The self-righteous justifications uttered by mill owners about these practices sound hollow now, but they went down well at the time, especially as the yarn produced was more regular than that formerly made by hand in cottages.

In time the factory system was introduced into most areas of textile manufacturing.

Worsted

Long and short staple wool were spun and woven in different ways. Worsted is a tough fabric made from long staple wool which has been combed to remove its tendency to felt. Long staple wool was much more suited to machine spinning and so the production of worsted was mechanised decades before that of short staple wool.

West Riding towns such as Huddersfield changed from kerseys to making worsted as it became popular, but when the population rose few new weavers could find smallholdings to supplement their earnings and so were forced to

became full-time employees of the worsted masters, which made them vulnerable to wage cuts.

Cloth

'Cloth' was the name for fabric made from short staple wool. It did not lend itself to machine weaving and so although the yarn was spun in factories, the handloom weavers continued to work at home, often in cottages with ranges of windows in the upper floor to give them better light.

Most cloth firms were small, without either the capital or the inclination to mechanise weaving. The exception was Bean Ing Mill, a huge complex built by Benjamin Gott of Leeds, which was the first mill in the West Riding to have the new Boulton and Watt steam engines. The mill contained areas for all stages of cloth production, from scribbling (straightening the wool before carding) to finishing. Thousands of workers were employed there.

By the 1840s machines adapted for weaving cloth had been invented and although handloom weaving and its way of life did not disappear immediately, it was on its way out.

> Where are the girls? I will tell you, son,
> The girls are gone to weave by steam,
> And if you would see them you must rise at dawn,
> And trudge to the mill in the early morn!

(Folk song, 'The Handloom Weaver')

In the middle of the nineteenth century, the West Riding textile industry was the most prosperous in Europe. It attracted workers from all over the county, despite the conditions of work. Down the Calder Valley cloth towns soon crammed the spaces between factories. At Holmfirth, rows of terraced houses very different from the old detached weaver's cottages clustered along the sides of the hills, while in Hebden Bridge new houses were so tightly packed on the

steep banks above the river that they were partly on top of each other ('flying freeholds', hated by lawyers!).

Problems associated with overcrowding – bad sanitation, water pollution and disease – grew with the population. Bradford was characterised as 'the dirtiest, filthiest and worst-regulated town in the kingdom' by a Health of Towns commissioner. The average life expectancy was just 20, an average brought down by the appalling infant mortality.

IRON AND STEEL

By the nineteenth century coke, made from purified coal, was improving both steel and iron products. The leading ironmasters in northern England were those former Sheffield nailers, the Walker brothers. By this time they owned the largest steelworks in Europe and produced armaments for both the Revolutionary and Napoleonic wars. The business did not do well in peacetime, however, especially when the iron ore began to run out.

Further north in the Bradford district there was not only ironstone, but low-sulphur coal suitable for coking. An ironworks established at Birkenshaw and another at Low Moor continued to make wrought iron until 1957. Their products were exported around the world.

The Sheffield steel industry continued to grow until by the middle of the century it made 90 per cent of British steel and half of Europe's. Thanks to its crucible steel, Sheffield soon overtook London as England's pre-eminent cutlery centre. Handicrafts were still at the heart of the trade and most cutlery businesses were still small, though the Sheaf Works, built in 1823 by Messrs Greaves, was a self-contained factory, producing razors, penknives and such small goods for the American trade. By 1800 most of the entire world's cutlery was made in Sheffield.

CANALS AND RAILWAYS

The success of the improved river navigations and new canals inspired more ambitious schemes. Crossing the Pennines remained a challenge, but – with considerable trouble – two more canals, the Rochdale (to Halifax) and the Huddersfield (to Aston-under-Lyne) were constructed. The Standedge (pronounced Stannige) Tunnel on the Huddersfield Narrow Canal is the longest on any canal. It was opened in 1811 after years of technical trouble and lack of contractors willing to take on the apparently impossible task. Thomas Telford, the great engineer, was asked for his advice and he produced a detailed and costed plan that helped to reassure investors.

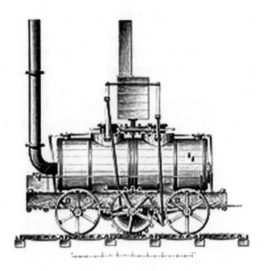

In the East Riding three canals linked the market towns of Pocklington, Driffield and Market Weighton to navigable rivers, and in the Vale of York the small town of Goole was developed into a canal port with docks by the construction of the Knottingley and Goole Canal, which improved the route to the Ouse.

Richard Trevithick's experiments with locomotives at Coalbrookdale opened the railway era, but its development was slow until 1811 when Matthew Murray of Fenton, Murray and Wood, in Holbeck, near Leeds, designed a locomotive (possibly called *Salamanca*) based on Richard Trevithick's locomotive, *Catch Me Who Can*, using a rack and pinion system devised by engineer John Blenkinsop. In this innovative system a pinion is meshed with a rack, thus allowing it to pull more weight. *Salamanca* subsequently moved coal from the Middleton quarry to the staithes on the Aire and Calder navigation.

Although the original purpose of railways was to move coal more easily, once it was realised that the public were keen to experience rail travel (and would pay for the privilege), it was only a matter of time before railways were carrying passengers. The first public-carrying railway was the Stockton and Darlington in 1825 (though the public coaches were initially pulled along the rails by horses – just in case!).

It was soon possible to travel by train all the way from London to Derby, Rotherham and York in hours rather than days. Railway fever began to grip the country and small railway companies, following Yorkshire's lead, sprang up all over the country. Most were too insufficiently capital-ised to invest in the unified system that was needed to create an efficient service. Small railway companies meant incon-venience for passengers who had to get out and purchase new tickets every time the end of that particular company's territory was reached. Many investors came from up-and-coming, newly middle-class families with plenty of money but no experience of finance. Their investments provided the essential money for financing the expensive business of building railways across the country, but they were invest-ing in a bubble and many had little return on their money except bankruptcy.

Step up George Hudson, the Railway King! Hudson, dynamic and unscrupulous, had met and been inspired by George Stephenson and his vision of an integrated railway. He had been left a fortune and was able to buy up failed railway companies cheap, setting up the York and North Midland Railway company in 1836 under his own chair-manship. Over time, the Y&NMR opened or took over other companies, eventually merging with several other large companies to form the Midland Railway. York's first station, wooden, was rebuilt in 1839 by the Y&NMR, inconveniently breaching the city's walls to allow trains access. The present station was built outside the walls much later, in 1877. It was partly thanks to Hudson that York became a great railway hub. He is still a well-known figure in York, despite being disgraced, eventually, for financial mismanagement verging on fraud by politician George Leeman, whose somewhat censorious statue standing somewhat gloomily near the arch in the breached walls through which the early trains ran. In his glory days he built a house on the Londesborough estate once owned by Burlington.

The most ambitious railway engineering project of the early nineteenth century was the Woodhead Tunnel, which provided a link between Sheffield and Manchester through the Pennines. It was over 3 miles long and over 1,500 navvies worked on it day and night, seven days a week. It was extremely dangerous for the workers, thirty-two of whom were killed by falling rocks or explosions. The navvies, well-paid but notoriously riotous after receiving their wages (which were only paid about every three months, to stop them running off), lived with their families in squalid huts at the Yorkshire end of the tunnel at Dunford Bridge and Woodend where disease was rife. A Parliamentary inquiry into their employment led to better conditions when a second tunnel was built alongside the first in 1847–52.

COAL MINING

The main coalfield in Yorkshire, the South Yorkshire coalfield, stretches from Halifax in the north west, to the north of Bradford and Leeds in the north east, Huddersfield and Sheffield in the west, and Doncaster in the east. With the advent of steam-powered factories and other engines, coal, hitherto a matter of small, shallow mines, became an attractive business for entrepreneurs, aristocratic as well as common. The Duke of Norfolk owned several collieries in Yorkshire and, wishing to improve their efficiency, asked his engineer, John Curr, to design new ways of moving coal in mines; up to that time it had been pushed on sledges. Curr invented large corves (trucks) which could run on iron plates. A rival aristocrat, William, the fourth Earl Fitzwilliam, already one of the greatest landowners in England, succeeded to a huge inheritance including the Wentworth Woodhouse and Malton estates. He and his son, Charles, believed that God not only gave the upper classes their wealth but also the responsibility to care for their tenants. Unlike many other mine owners, they were outstanding employers. They built rows of fine miners' cottages at Elsecar, where they sank a new pit to make use of the recently completed Dearne and Dove Canal. Elsecar also had a Miners' Lodging House, a Wesleyan chapel, a school, a flour mill and the Earl's private railway station.

Such aristocratic paternalism was lacking in many other mining towns where the lucrative demand for coal drove colliery owners to follow the Barnsley seam (which provided the best coal) as it dipped down further eastwards. The cost of deeper pits made it cheaper to sink them in open fields rather than under towns where pillars of coal had to be left to prevent the buildings above collapsing. Rows of cheap miners' cottages were built near the pit heads on those open fields too far from town for the miners to travel easily. New Sharleston near Wakefield is a good example.

Deeper pits meant more firedamp (methane) and more accidents, which until this time had been few. In the next two generations the death toll rose shockingly: the explosion at Oaks Colliery in 1847 killed seventy-three men; seventy-five died at Darley Main. At Husker Pit near Silkstone, twenty-six children, whose job it was to prevent firedamp building up by opening ventilation doors as a corf came along, were drowned when a storm flooded the pit.

Public horror at this last disaster led to a commission into child labour in mines. It found that the door openers, called 'trappers', were often children as young as 5 or 6, who sat in complete darkness. Others, employed as 'hurriers', pushed the loaded corves up to the bottom of the shaft. At Foster Place Colliery near Hepworth, where there were no rails, girls 'dressed like boys in trousers, with belts around their waists and chains passing between their legs' had to pull the corves on all fours; 'one of the most disgusting sights I have ever seen', said a commissioner. The upshot was an

Act passed in 1842 prohibiting the employment in mines of all females, and boys under the age of 10.

THE RISE OF OPPOSITION

In 1843 a Miners' Association was formed to fight for better wages. They decided to demonstrate at Hood Hall near Chapeltown. The employers, really alarmed when 4,000 men attended, agreed together to exclude in future any employee who joined the Association. Strikes broke out all over the coalfield and in 1844 most of the West Riding colliers stopped work. One of the owners retaliated by evicting all strikers from the houses he rented to them. The strike was broken as a result and the Association lapsed. Its ideas had not, however, and in 1858 miners from coalfields all over the country got together to form the Miners' Association of the United Kingdom. The bitterness against employers that was such a legacy of this period remained, building up trouble for future years.

Many families had benefitted from good wages in the textile trades as long as skilled workers were in demand, and so when machines began to take over their jobs workers fought hard to stop them. Croppers and shearmen in the West Riding, skilled men who 'finished' the cloth, fought the introduction of new shearing machines which required only one worker – or even a child – to watch each one, instead of four skilled men. Suddenly they were no longer valued workers but lowly operatives.

The new machinery was introduced in the early years of the century at a particularly bad time because there had been a considerable rise in the cost of food following the Napoleonic Wars, and many poor workers were starving. A secret society, the so-called Luddites (named after a mythical British king, Ludd), began to break up the new machines, at first winning a lot of sympathy from respectable citizens, who felt uneasy about the working classes being deprived of work. In April 1812, 300 men set fire to the mill of Joseph Foster and the attackers of William Cartwright's mill in Spen valley had to be driven off with muskets. Public sympathy began to wane and when, in the same year, a mill owner from Ottiwells near Halifax was shot dead by Luddites it was felt that severe action must be taken. Seventeen Luddites were subsequently hanged at York and seven transported to Australia.

The next twenty years saw the rise of demands for votes for all (men) and increased political activity in the working classes. Better understanding of the plight of those who had no say in government and a better-informed public who had mostly supported the Slavery Abolition Act of 1833 seem to have illuminated the cruelty of working conditions in the textile mills; some even compared its workers to slaves. In 1830 the *Leeds Mercury* printed a letter from Richard Oastler, a man who managed to combine being a Tory supporter of the Duke of Wellington with being a radical and abolitionist. He condemned 'those magazines [storehouses] of British infantile slavery, the worsted mills of the town and neighbourhood of Bradford'. His concerns were echoed by others of his class, Tory landowners who feared unrest and wished to restore the old social order. They founded the Ten Hours Movement to limit the length of the working day in mills. Though they were fiercely opposed by mill owners, in the end a royal commission, shocked by what was revealed in interviews with employees, supported an Act prohibiting the employment of children under the age of 9, and limiting the hours of older children and teenagers. In 1847 the Ten Hours Act was passed.

RURAL LIFE

It is a relief to turn from the turmoil of the industrial towns to the peaceful life in the countryside, which continued in its quiet way throughout this period. Changes came but they were few compared with what had happened in towns. Machinery was not yet revolutionising the farm, although horse-drawn reapers and threshers were being invented. Horses and oxen were still the main suppliers of power.

Many of the farming population still practiced other crafts, and although knitting and linen weaving had declined, lead mining on the moors flourished, with its peak in the middle of the nineteenth century.

The Enclosures that had been such a feature of the middle and late eighteenth century continued into the nine-teenth. It changed the look of the land in the Wolds, but even more particularly in the Dales. In moorland areas miles of straight gritstone walls divided fields into neat rectangles, even climbing pointlessly straight up steep hills. These walls were not to keep stock in, but, like the haw-thorn hedges in the Wolds, were demanded of their owners (sometimes in tedious detail) by the Acts that enclosed the land. Farmsteads and barns were erected in the new fields: the characteristic Dales two-storey Dales barn standing alone is a product of enclosure. The unfarmable moorland on the tops, not worth walling, remained in use for sheep runs, or was sometimes turned into grouse moors, all rights of public access removed.

On a more positive note, the disappearance of common-ers' rights meant that landowners could now engage in drainage projects not possible before; places like Wallingfen were drained and turned into arable.

Small industries were common in most market towns. By the middle of the century Driffield, for example, had two mills for crushing bones for manure, 'commodious wharfs and warehouses', an iron foundry, a tannery and looms for carpets, sacking and linen. Most villages of any size were still self-sufficient in crafts, with tailors, shoe- and dress-makers, haberdashers, builders and other 'small mesters' capable of turning their hands to a variety of jobs. Brewing and baking were a local affair. The local baker's oven provided not just bread, but a baking service for the many inhabitants who had no oven. Even in the West Riding there were still rural villages where life went on as before, with small family businesses such as basket-weaving, glass-making and pottery side by side with farming.

Meanwhile, rural Yorkshire had entered the public's consciousness through the books of the Brontë sisters. Inspired by Emily's description of the wild romantic moors – or perhaps hoping to meet their own Heathcliff (or Cathy) – visitors began to come in some numbers. Mrs Gaskell's biography of Charlotte Brontë added further details of her tragic life (while suppressing less creditable ones), rescuing her reputation from the accusation of being 'unwomanly' and inspiring interest in visiting Haworth. A tentative tourist industry had begun. (Visitors appear to have been unconcerned about catching the TB that caused the death of their heroines!)

Another author, Charles Dickens, publicised something not nearly as much to the credit of the county as its countryside: the existence of the infamous Yorkshire cheap boarding schools. *Nicholas Nickleby*, based on Dickens' own visit to such a school (in Bowes) revealed a place where unwanted children could be placed a long way from their relations and forgotten (with 'no vacations'). The reality

EDUCATION.—At Mr. CLARKSON'S Old-established CLASSICAL, COMMERCIAL and MATH-EMATICAL ACADEMY, Bowes-hall, near Greta Bridge, Yorkshire, BOYS are Boarded, provided with books, &c. and expeditiously instructed in every branch of a useful and polite Education, necessary to qualify them for any situation in life, at 20 guineas a year: the French Language is taught in its greatest purity, by a native of France, at 10s. 6d. per quarter. Mr. C. pledges himself that the strictest attention is paid to the health, moral conduct and intellectual improvement of his Pupils; and in order to expedite their Education as much as possible, he teaches assiduously in the School himself, and does not allow any vacations. For cards, and reference to parents of boys educated at this establishment, apply to Mr. Smith, 26. Lombard-street, who is Mr. C.'s agent, and will give information respecting the conveyance from London to Bowes-hall.

was as bad as the book makes out. Often starved or used as cheap labour and vulnerable to do whatever the so-called masters desired, the wretched pupils' only plan was to survive long enough to grow up and escape.

> Every other morning we used to flea the beds. The usher used to cut the quills, and give us them to catch the fleas; and if you did not fill the quill, you caught a good beating. The pot-skimmings were called broth, and we used to have it for tea on Sunday.
>
> (Quote from a pupil)

Dickens' novel did the job its author intended and destroyed the Yorkshire School industry.

THE POOR

'The poor are always with us,' says the Bible. The poor and destitute certainly increased considerably during the nineteenth century and their misery in cities was great, as any reader of Charles Dickens knows. Fortunately for the poor of Yorkshire, they had things rather better than that in London or counties further south.

To begin with, their diet, if dull, was better. Most people had meat a couple of times a week, milk, butter, potatoes and that drink once only enjoyed by the rich but now universal, tea, for breakfast. Even after the bad harvests of 1795 and 1801 the death toll from starvation was minimal, with public and private relief and self-help societies taking on the job of providing food.

There were very few people in the Yorkshire workhouses – only three in Driffield, all well-cared for, according to visitors. When times were bad and people laid off, ratepayers seem to have been much more understanding than in other counties, providing outdoor relief to families with a reasonably good grace. They probably knew that better times would quickly remove the burden as people were re-employed. Wages were, in any case, higher than in the south, even for farm labourers, allowing thrifty people to save a small amount for rainy days.

All this didn't mean that life was easy. Poverty was harsh in times of depression such as after the Napoleonic Wars when many people (particularly from the North Riding) were forced to seek work in America and Canada.

The population increase inevitably led to an unwelcome rise in the Poor Rates nationally so that by the 1800s Parliament was turning its attention to ways of reducing the burden. A poisonous cocktail of self-interest, hypocrisy, misguided theories about population and sheer distrust of the poor produced the Poor Law Amendment Act of 1834. All outdoor relief was banned; all paupers were to be sent instead to the workhouse, which should be made as unpleasant as possible so that it became 'an object of wholesome horror'. Families were to be broken up intentionally. Many people thought that it was the Act that was the object of horror. Riots broke out, nowhere more fiercely than in Yorkshire where the old Elizabethan Poor Law still worked well with the fluctuations of work, tiding people over during difficult periods. An Anti-Poor Law Amendment Movement was organised in the West Riding and riots broke out. Yorkshire objectors pointed out that there were no workhouses existing in the county that could contain all those who would need to be put in them in bad times, and that building them would not just be expensive but pointless, as in good times they would be empty. Full implementation of the new Act was quietly dropped in Yorkshire, though not in other counties.

DISSENTERS, METHODISM AND CHURCHGOING

In 1665 the Act of Uniformity removed any vicar who refused to accept the practices of the Church of England. Those who would not were called dissenters. Their objections were mostly based on their opposition to state interference in religious matters. They were a small but contentious lot, splitting into as many as seventeen different small sects (though many had disappeared by the nineteenth century). Dissenters were not very common to begin with, but in the moors and the large lowland parishes with links to Hull and in some towns like Wakefield and Sheffield they quietly increased. Wakefield produced Quakers who 'quaked' at the power of God. They included some of the ironmasters of the West Riding, and were the most widespread of the dissenters to begin with; the great Yorkshire chocolate manufacturers and philanthropists Rowntree and Terry were descended from them.

As the eighteenth century grew older the 'enthusiasm' (religious inspiration) of previous years cooled and more secular interests took over. The Wesley brothers and George Whitefield set out to remedy this, preaching first in rural areas before venturing into towns, where they did not always meet with success: 'we have also preached at Barnsley,' a follower reported, 'where they were very angry and cast rotten eggs at us ...'

Churchgoing numbers were very low in towns at this time, the Church of England having snored in lazy prosperity for a century. Most of the urban working classes probably preferred to spend their one day off a week in some other, warmer, way, but there were those who were inspired by the simple message of Wesleyan Methodism which focused on the possibility of salvation for all, and the need for practicing charity. Its strong musical traditions appealed as well, as did its practical emphasis on the working- and middle-class virtues of self-improvement, thrift and hard work. The Wesleyan Movement began to grow, particularly in the West Riding. It soon had more adherents than the Church of England, which woke with a start and engaged in a burst of church building.

Methodists were not the only non-conforming group trying to gain converts and they themselves split into sub-sects such as Primitive Methodists. You can find small chapels of different, once-competing denominations, now mostly turned into houses, scattered throughout the towns and villages of Yorkshire, sometimes next to one another.

YORKSHIRE FOLK:

John Atkinson Grumshaw (1836-1893) was an important Victorian painter, born in Leeds, famous for his city night scenes and landscapes. He was greatly influenced by the realism of the Pre-Raphaelites and his paintings are vividly detailed realistic depictions of the moonlight scenes he particularly loved. His pictures of suburban streets and the docks in London, Hull, Liverpool and Glasgow are notable for their mood, colour and lighting.

PLACES TO VISIT:

Haworth Village: West Yorkshire. Worth visiting to add to the Brontë experience

National Coal Mining Museum: Caphouse Colliery, New Road, Wakefield, West Yorkshire

Elsecar Heritage Centre: Wath Road, Elsecar, Barnsley, South Yorkshire

Leeds Industrial Museum: For textiles in particular. Canal Road, Leeds, West Yorkshire

16

THE HEIGHT
OF EMPIRE

The Great Exhibition of 1851 marked a high point in the British Empire. Designed to display the wealth, power and manufacturing supremacy of Britain, its one million exhibits included thousands made by Yorkshire people. This was the age of an Empire 'on which the Sun never sets' but which exploited people at home and abroad. Cheap raw materials from the colonies around the world flowed into the county, were transformed into goods and sold back at a huge profit.

The population in the West Riding was now three and a half times that in the rest of the county. Workers were flowing in not just from Britain but from other countries too. Some 40,000 immigrants escaping the Irish Potato Famine took refuge here, congregating in the poorest parts of towns like Leeds and York. They provided a cheap source of power for major projects but were subjected to exploitation and abuse. Meanwhile, a series of pogroms and restrictive laws in Russia produced a large influx of Russian Jews, most of whom seem to have gone to Leeds, where they gave the clothes industry an enormous boost.

'Progress' was the word of the century. Inventers invented with no thought for the consequences; capital could be found for almost any project providing you could make the right contacts. It was a time when a bright young man could go far (a bright young woman had first to fight for financial and educational freedom).

RAILWAYS

Railways spectacularly transformed the landscape with viaducts, cuttings, embankments and tunnels during the second half of the nineteenth century. The 13-mile line from Pennistone to Huddersfield starts with a viaduct of twenty-nine arches over the Don and continues in the same exuberant style over Denby Dale's twenty-one huge arches. The Settle to Carlisle Railway, opened in 1875, is still the most spectacular (and probably the best-loved) in England, with its twenty-eight arched Ribblehead Viaduct designed by J.S. Crossley.

These amazing feats of engineering, built by a cheap labour force, were mostly created to facilitate the carriage of goods. Competition between coal towns was fierce: each tried to get its coal to a port before the others. Railway yards, the distribution centres of their day, sprang up near railway hubs like York with sidings for shunting goods-trucks covering many acres, and with engineering works nearby. The North East Railway opened the York Carriage Works in 1884. They employed over 1,500 people and only closed in 1996 after rail privatisation.

Doncaster eventually became one of the most important railway towns. It had the vast engineering works called 'the Plant'. By 1900 the works employed 4,500 men and covered 200 acres with 60 miles of sidings.

In Hull, where the present grand station was built by the NER, the coming of the railway facilitated more development. Hull was now the country's third largest port, with goods coming and going to Russia, Scandinavia, Denmark, Germany, Holland, Belgium and France. It now built two enormous new docks, the St Andrew and the Alexandra. Fishing continued to be important to the city and the St Andrew was the largest fish dock in the world, but it was the complex of railways that took its produce to the rest of England.

Many folk could now afford to take the train instead of the fast-vanishing stagecoach and even take the family on day trips to Bridlington or Scarborough. By the 1900s nearly every reasonably sized town (and quite a few small ones) was connected to a railway line.

IRON AND STEEL

Middlesbrough was founded in 1830 as a port from which the coal brought on the Stockton to Darlington railway could be exported. It had been transformed when that coal ran out and two men, the philanthropist Henry Bolckow and his associate, John Vaughan, persuaded the town to exploit the ironstone newly discovered in the Eston Hills and make iron. So successful was this change that the coal staithes had to be greatly enlarged to accommodate the enormous quantity of goods the port now handled. Soon the export of pig iron reached 2 million tons, about a third of British output. For a while, times and wages were good for Teeside workers and the town gained the nickname of 'Ironopolis', but, inevitably, the iron too began to run out and had to be imported. Middlesbrough adapted. In the 1870s, as sail started to give way to steam, the town began to make Bessemer and sheet steel for the new iron-clad ships. In later years the successful Teeside steel industry built both the New Tyne Bridge in Newcastle and the Sydney Harbour Bridge.

In Sheffield steel production had taken over from cutlery as the most important industry by the 1860s as first

Bessemer and then open-hearth furnaces were adopted. In the early days, rails for railways were important products, and exported widely, especially to America, but when railway building at home slowed down and America began to mine its own plentiful supplies of ironstone, Sheffield's foundries branched out into armaments. There were many arms manufacturers, household names in their day: Brown and Cammell's made armour plating; Firth's, guns; Hadfield's, shells; but chief of all was Vickers, which made all types of weapons. Although being overtaken in steel production by other industrialising countries like Germany and America, Sheffield remained world-class in the production of specialist steels. Most of the alloy steels were discovered there, manganese and stainless steel among them.

Sheffield's cutlery industry was still important, with well-known manufacturers such as Rogers and Co. and Mappin Bros. The Mappin family had long been in the business, becoming wealthy benefactors of the town. One of the younger members started an electroplating business with his brother-in-law George Webb to form the well-known firm of Mappin & Webb Cutlery. His elder brother, Fred, founded the Technical School and the University as well as leaving eighty pictures to the Mappin Art Gallery.

COAL

The success of Victorian industry was founded on coal. During the second half of the nineteenth century production in the Yorkshire and North Midland coalfield increased from 8 million to 73 million tons.

Many of the more than 94,000 coalminers recorded as living in the West Riding were in new settlements or vastly expanded old villages such as Wath upon Dearne. Ever-growing spoil heaps dominated the landscape.

Miners from the Black Country flowed in to find work in the Yorkshire pits as their own became exhausted, and in the 1871 census over half the population of Low Valley came from outside Yorkshire.

Safety had not improved much since the terrible mining disasters of the 1840s. The Oaks Pit was, once again, the site of a terrible explosion in 1866, from which only six of the 340 miners working at the time escaped. It could be heard 3 miles away. The safety recommendations about ventilation made after the previous disaster had been ignored, despite complaints from the miners only a few days before the accident. To make matters worse, twenty-one of the rescuers were killed in a second explosion the following day.

In 1868 a new pit was sunk near Mexborough by a hard-headed group of West Riding coal owners. The pit was called Donaby Main ('main' indicating that it was on the Barnsley seam). A village was built next to it with the type of parallel streets of terraced two-up, two-down houses, all owned by the mining company, that remains in the public mind as the very image of a Yorkshire pit village. In 1899 the Christian Budget characterised Danaby Main as the 'Worst Village in England', 'where nearly all the men and most of the women devote their high wages to betting ... where wives are sold like cattle and children neglected'.

Industrialists had by this time learned to fear the combined strike power of their workers: there was little love lost on either side and masters no longer hesitated to inflict harm to keep their large workforces in order.

Most of the workers at Danaby came from outside Yorkshire and were already hardened by conflicts at other pits. Trouble broke out in the following year when the owners sacked any man who had joined a union. Three hundred and fifty miners went on strike in sympathy and were all sacked and evicted, but in the end financial pressures meant that the owners had to admit defeat. More strikes occurred in subsequent years. The Miners' Federation of Great Britain faced its biggest test when, in 1893, 300,000 miners were locked out for refusing to accept a 25 per cent reduction in wages to offset a drop in the price of coal (not for the last time). There was violence and two men were killed when the Militia, called out to quell riots, opened fire. The miners won, however, just as they were to do in 1912 when a million went on strike for a minimum wage.

It was because of the existence of such places as Danaby that the theories of Socialism described by Robert Owen had been passed on and discussed by two generations of middle- and working-class people. Then, towards the last quarter of the century, Keir Hardy, a miner from Owen's old stamping-ground in Lanarkshire made a bid to be elected to Parliament. Hardy, though closely involved with the Union Movement, realised that if working people were to be helped it would have to be through legislation. After initial failure, he was finally elected as member for West Ham – and duly appeared in the House wearing, to the horror of frock-coated, top-hatted members, a red tie and a deerstalker.

Feeling that the Liberal Party, which was the only Opposition party at the time, was not sufficiently on the side of working men, he joined with others (particularly men from the Yorkshire Unions) to form the Labour Party in 1900.

The Conservative Party had been in power for years, becoming more and more unpopular. The Liberals, fearing to lose yet again at the approaching 1905 elections, formed a pact with Labour supporters (engineered by Hardy's fellow Scot and Socialist, Ramsay MacDonald) agreeing not to stand against each other. Union and Socialist activists all over Yorkshire and other counties, while not necessarily agreeing with everything the new party stood for, supported them and helped to produce not just a huge landslide win for the Liberals but twenty new Labour MPs.

The Liberal government with its Labour help passed the most revolutionary legislation for working people of any previous government. The most important Act, as far as ordinary folk were concerned, was the creation of old-age pensions and unemployment insurance. Now elderly people no longer had to fear being separated from their partners in the workhouse. Equally ground-breaking was the Parliament Act 1911, which removed the law-making veto from the House of Lords, thereby making the House of Commons the more important legislating body.

A few years later the first fully Labour government, with MacDonald as its first Prime Minister, took its seats.

RURAL LIFE

There are still elderly people living who can speak 'Yorkshire', though fewer every year. The old words and syntax remained in use in country districts until the present century, but even in the middle of the nineteenth century pressure from education, a desire to better oneself and population movements were changing the speech, not just of Yorkshire, but the whole of England. Regional accents were now frowned on and children were stopped (often by physical punishment) from using dialect words.

For a while the old beliefs and traditions hung on in rural districts: fairies danced near moor villages; witches stole milk from cows; and wise men revealed the identity of thieves and wrought wonderful cures. Folk 'told the bees' about a death or insisted that coffins could be taken to the graveyard only along corpse roads. A new interest in 'Old Ways' meant that some of these things were recorded, but much more was lost forever, and more still was probably never revealed to the clever 'educated' men who wanted to collect it.

An increasing distance was opening up between rich landowners and their tenants. Estates in some parts of Yorkshire had become so vast that few landowners spent much time mixing with the lower orders in the way their grandparents had felt it their duty to do. On the

Wolds the Sykes estate was over 34,000 acres and that of Londesborough 33,000, while the Stricklands owned 20,000. Sir Tatton Sykes, a famous Wolds figure, had ridden to hounds and boxed with his tenants, but his son and grandson kept themselves more aloof, spending much time in London.

In the eighteenth century, aristocrats were often to be seen enjoying working-class activities which gave them relief from the demands of polite society, but the new middle classes took themselves far more seriously: they were greatly concerned with appearance and behaviour. This often took the form of trying to restrict anything that might encourage drunkenness or rowdy behaviour. Old traditions, such as church ales (jolly drinking parties), were often stopped on the grounds of taste. One of the traditions which came under fire was the Martinmas hiring fair, where young men and women looking for farm work stood in the market place waiting for a prospective employer. Such fairs took place all over rural East Yorkshire and were often accompanied by a fair amount of drunkenness and jollity as the young folk celebrated what was one of their few opportunities to be in each other's company for a week and spend the 'fest penny', a small sum that 'fastened' them to their new employer.

These fairs, which lasted a week and were also attended by all types of entertainers, cheap jacks and so on, often became noisy, offending more respectable people. The Church was particularly opposed to the whole business of hiring on an annual basis because farm servants were, on the whole, not churchgoers and considered to have degenerate morals. Serious attempts were made by clergymen in the East Riding to end the fairs or at least separate the sexes into hiring rooms but they failed: the system worked and neither farmers nor the farm servants themselves wanted it to change. Driffield hiring fair, notoriously riotous, continued well until the twentieth century, although by then the hiring aspect had disappeared.

Although traditional farming practices continued in hill farms, machinery was now being introduced. Seed drills, steam ploughs and many types of horse-drawn winnowers, hoes and reapers appeared in more wealthy areas. Wire fencing, oil cake for cattle and chemical fertilisers all began to be adopted.

Farming prosperity was high in the 1860s because of demand in the industrial towns, but this changed when Russia on the steppes and America in the prairies began growing wheat. Soon the market became saturated with wheat and the price plummeted, hitting Holderness and the Wolds hard. A second blow to Wolds farmers came when Australia began exporting quantities of merino wool, cheaper and of better quality than they could themselves produce.

In later years refrigerated imported meat and dairy imports provided even more competition for farmers, but the sheer quality of their beef and mutton kept many a Yorkshire farm in business.

TEXTILE TOWNS

Continuous changes in fashion and the use of new materials, such as mohair, kept the textile industry on its toes. In the Huddersfield district, which produced a wider range of fabrics than any other place, mills now wove not just fashionable fancy cloths in intricate designs, but the plain twills that Americans preferred.

'Where there's muck there's brass.' This well-known Yorkshire saying could be applied to the production of the cloth called 'shoddy'. It involved the recycling of old woollen clothes by shredding them and recovering the wool. It sounds clean enough, but given that woollen clothes were worn unwashed and handed down until

they virtually fell apart, and given the low hygiene standards of ordinary people during the nineteenth century, it is not surprising that it was described as 'a very filthy trade'. Dirty it might have been, but it was also very lucrative and shoddy (which had not yet acquired its modern meaning) mixed with different fibres was widely worn.

Most textile towns diversified into other trades as the century progressed. Halifax became known as 'the city of a hundred trades'. It ventured into financial services, particularly building societies, which had grown out of the old Friendly Societies that supported poor workers. The Halifax Permanent Building Society was founded in 1853.

Leeds also moved away from its textile past as its engineering, leather and chemical industries expanded. John Fowler manufactured traction engines and steam ploughs in the 1850s, and by 1893 engineers in the city had advanced to making locomotives and rolling stock as well as other specialist machinery. The clothing trade took off, employing thousands of women who had previously worked in the flax industry. Sewing machines, introduced in 1855, improved the speed of work and hundreds of them were installed in small cramped sweatshops, where their operators often worked in unhealthy conditions for a pittance.

Leeds was by now a smoky, dirty place, but its city council and wealthier citizens tried to improve its appearance by building the imposing new town hall and acquiring the Roundhay estate as a healthful park for citizens. Culture was regarded as an important sign of a town's greatness, and Leeds was not going to be found wanting: the first Leeds Music Festival was held in 1858, and it was followed by the building of public libraries, the Art Gallery and the Yorkshire College, which was to become Leeds University.

Some of the main streets, residential no longer, were cleared and widened at the end of the century, allowing entrepreneurs to rebuild with large shops and, the latest thing, department stores, luring in customers with fancy displays, electric lifts and elegant tearooms. Alexander Monteith's Grand Pygmalion, at the corner of Boar Lane and Briggate, employed 200 assistants on four floors. It sold everything from mantles to sunshades, millinery, corsets, ladies' boots, gentlemen's hosiery, bedding, carpets, china, children's costumes, haberdashery, bedsteads and much more, all displayed with 'consummate taste and effect!'

Rivalry between towns was still keen. The monumental civic buildings that characterise so many English towns (and for which it is now so difficult to find uses) were mostly built at this period. At the height of its Victorian pride, Bradford not only dealt with its infrastructure problems but built St George's Hall (containing a concert hall, restaurant and galleries), two theatres, two music halls and numerous civic buildings.

The same architects, the firm of Lockwood & Mawson, which designed many of Bradford's buildings, were also chosen to design the model village at Saltaire for mill-owner Titus Salt. They were told to combine 'every improvement

that modern art and science have brought to light'. Salt
had mohair and alpaca weaving mills and was Bradford's
Mayor in 1848. The model village had 150 houses for the
workers, along with churches, a school and an institute, but
no pubs (it became a World Heritage Site in 2001).

HOUSING

The philanthropic motives that drove many reformers in
the late nineteenth century did not just provide theories but
extended to such practical aspects as disposal of sewage and
the provision of clean water. A better understanding of disease (as the medical profession emerged from centuries of
deluded ignorance) led to a feeling of urgency as outbreaks
of cholera became more virulent and their causes clearer.
(Victims from York's cholera outbreak lie in their own cemetery just outside the station.) The well-known response of
Parliament to the summer of the 'Great Stink' in 1858 was to
initiate the building of the great Victorian sewage system on
which London still relies, but other cities dragged their feet
because of the logistical difficulties and cost.

Sheffield was a particularly unhealthy place with a death
rate from contagious diseases higher than any other town
in England. Smoke added to its health problems. John
Murray's *Handbook for Travellers in Yorkshire* (1867)
says that:

> Sheffield ... the largest and most important town in Yorkshire, is
> beyond all question the blackest, dirtiest and least agreeable. It is
> indeed impossible to walk through the streets without suffering
> from the dense clouds of smoke constantly pouring from great
> open furnaces in and around the town.

The city contained thousands of back-to-back houses (their
building was banned in 1864), built cheaply by local specu-
lators. The council did not have either the money or the

authority to remove such houses and build others. They were still there by the First World War. Other towns had the same disincentives.

In 1901, Benjamin Seebohm Rowntree published the influential *Poverty: A Study of Town Life* about York. Rowntree was a member of the famous Quaker sweet family. His book was one of the first in-depth studies of the poor. A similar detailed study of Middlesbrough was produced by Lady Florence Bell ten years later. Rowntree's company went further and built York's first garden village at New Earswick. There was mixed housing for both workers and managers, in a green setting with gardens for each home with its own two fruit trees. Rowntree rejected paternalism, saying, 'I do not want to establish communities bearing the stamp of charity but rather of rightly ordered and self-governing communities.'

Even though wholesale redevelopment was not yet a possibility, many towns made a big effort to help their citizens, creating hospitals (including isolation hospitals for contagious diseases and others for sick children), and asylums for the mentally ill, as well as setting up sewage farms and improving the water supply.

While the middle classes escaped from increasingly dirty town centres to healthier new suburbs, the aristocracy was spending more time either in Town (i.e. London) or in warmer climes abroad. They preferred updating their Georgian houses, adding modern features such as conservatories or walled gardens, to building grand new houses. Exceptions in Yorkshire are Allerton Park, built in the Gothic style for Lord Bourton, and Brodsworth in South Yorkshire. The latter is the most complete example of a Victorian country house, surrounded by a formal garden. It is now in the care of Historic England.

Domestic life was made easier and healthier with the spread of gas for cooking and lighting. Electricity began to be used for street lighting, and Bradford built the first municipal power station, but its uptake in homes was slow – possibly due to well-justified suspicion of its safety.

Telephone history was made by a Yorkshire vicar, Revd Henry Hunnings of Bolton Percy, who invented a new type of transmitter that was to become the standard instrument of the Bell Companies. Telephones began to be used nationally in about 1878, though only the rich could afford them.

Most towns had piped water by the end of the century and water closets were the norm. Copper boilers heated by coal fires beneath, or kettles on the stove, were the sources of hot water for most people: the water-heating systems of the aristocracy were far too expensive (and large) for most houses. Washing machines hadn't got much further than a paddle in a barrel, and the steamy wash day with its damp atmosphere of drying washing remained for many decades yet.

Proper bathrooms existed only in the houses of the more wealthy: most people had their one bath a week in a tin bath in front of the fire (often sharing the water!).

PASTIMES

The common pastimes of the eighteenth century had mostly been masculine (and often violent): hunting, racing, boxing, dog- and cock-fighting, gambling. By the late Victorian period such activities (with the exception of racing) were thought of as vulgar or only suitable for the working orders. Gentlemen and ladies preferred (or at least said they did) more aesthetic pursuits: the theatre and arts, concerts, doing good.

Women having been absent from the pages of most of this book – history has been told by men – it is gratifying to record that they were finally beginning to stand up for themselves and take back some power. A sign of the changing times was the Married Women's Property Act 1882 which significantly altered English law, allowing married women to own and control property in their own right, while the rise of the Suffragette Movement, later in the century, was a natural development of the thoughts on justice and equality that had been floating around since the beginning of the century.

Generations of super-confident men (many of whom had opposed even the *male* franchise let alone votes for females) had laughed at the women who wanted to take part in the government of their own country by voting. As the Suffragette movement really got going, branches sprang up in Yorkshire towns: Yorkshire women were not going to be left out! They were often mill workers also involved in the trade union movement which saw getting votes for women as part of a larger campaign for equality. It should not be forgotten that they were supported by many working men who appreciated the heavy burden shouldered by working women with families.

One of the most well-known was Dora Thewlis, a weaver from Huddersfield and an active member of her local branch of the Women's Social and Political Union, which supported the Suffragette cause. When Dora went down to London to take part in one of their protests, her iconic photograph, showing her being restrained by two policemen – her shawl askew, a defiant expression on her face – made it on to the front page of a national newspaper. The photo was subsequently turned into a Suffragette propaganda postcard, much to her embarrassment.

The franchise was granted to women over the age of 30 in 1918 and over 21 in 1928.

The invention of the bicycle allowed the daring female to escape the boring round of polite tea-drinking and head off (still corseted) into the wild countryside. Some even took to smoking or (only in country houses where they could not be seen by the public) playing billiards and tennis.

Ideas on exercise for women was split between those who thought it was important for health and those who feared that, like too much education, it would somehow interfere with the childbearing parts. Women themselves were a little hesitant as to how much they could do. They only began to play tennis and golf in public just before the First World War. However, they were represented at the second Olympic Games which took place in France. Twenty-two women from different countries competed in sailing, tennis, croquet, equestrian and golf.

The dead hand of respectability was against the more lively pleasures of the poor. However, the poor, particularly the poor of Yorkshire (who thought themselves as good as their masters), were quite capable of standing up for themselves. Anglican clergymen did not help their religious cause by arrogantly intervening in traditional pleasures, especially as some appeared to think that nothing except work and humble churchgoing was suitable for the working family.

Despite this, many new entertainments were now on offer to tempt the pocket of the better-paid working family. Music halls were extremely popular. These places spent money on their décor to attract those whose days were often spent in smoky gloom and dirt. Bradford's Empire Music Hall, which offered light entertainment in exotic surroundings, told its potential audience that 'the illumination is by twenty Oriental lamps and lounges and other accessories are provided'. There were also verses, said to be in Arabic, decorating the walls. The Alhambra (named after the Emir's palace in Granada) was built in 1913 and continued the exotic 'Eastern' theme popular at the time.

Rather more highbrow music was (and is still) to be heard at the magnificent Leeds Grand Opera House, which was built in 1878. Its interior was also designed with an Eastern theme, Indian this time, and is one of the finest in Britain.

York obviously felt the need for a similar attraction, but York's days of prosperity were long behind it and its Grand Theatre and Opera House is in fact a warehouse and corn exchange cobbled together. Opened in 1902 it mostly showed films, despite its fancy name. There were a surprising number of full-length silent films made before the First World War as well as short comedies.

Films were also one of the attractions shown in booths at fairs. These continued to be popular, even though the days of the big animal fairs were over. They provided an excitedly awaited day out but they were not popular with respectable folk, always keen to control the working classes access to drink. In 1871 the respectable brigade managed to get the Fairs Act passed, which gave councils permission to abolish any fair in its area if:

It was unnecessary
It was the cause of gross immorality
It was very injurious to the inhabitants of the town in which it was held.

Several ancient fairs were closed under this Act, but Hull Fair, 700 years old and probably fulfilling all of the above qualifications, was supported by the inhabitants. It managed to survive to become the largest travelling fair in Europe today. In earlier days it had featured jugglers and theatrical and puppet shows, as well as Bostock and Wombwell's Menagerie, which introduced Hull folk to wild animals. In later years the Fair and the public took with enthusiasm to the new steam-powered roundabouts. A description of one of these merry-go-rounds was given in the *Halifax Courier* as a:

> roundabout of huge proportions, driven by a steam engine, which whirled around with such impetuosity, that the wonder is the daring riders are not shot off like cannon-balls, and driven half into the middle of next month.

Hull Fair was famous for its black boxers who challenged all comers. Black people were rare in Yorkshire, though Hull probably saw quite a few as they were commonly employed as sailors, and often married and raised families in English port towns. Boxing was a popular sailors' sport in seaports. The Hull boxers are immortalised in a short 1902 film, outside their booth at the Fair.

Travelling circuses like Gess's Managerie visited many parts of Yorkshire throughout the summer. Another, Mander's Royal Menagerie, featured a famous black lion tamer, Martini Maccomo, known as the Lion King, who appeared for some years to popular acclaim.

Railways now provided even working people with opportunities to go for day trips to different regions of the county. The wealthier might choose to visit Scarborough or Harrogate, which catered for them by building the Royal Baths. There, one could enjoy therapeutic baths and treatments in finely decorated rooms and then take a walk in the newly laid out Valley Pleasure Grounds or take tea in the thatched teahouse (in 1919 they could go to Betty's instead).

One of the ironies of the time was that because laws now restricted women's working hours and they no longer worked on Saturday afternoon, mill owners didn't find it economic to employ men to fill the extra hours and so they also got a half day's holiday. Both now had time to spend doing other things, and for men it was often playing sports of one kind or another.

The first rugby clubs had been formed down south in 1864 but the game soon caught on in Yorkshire, with clubs being formed all over the place in the 1870s and '80s. In 1895, however, there was a split. Twenty rebel clubs, including Leeds, Halifax, Wigan and Widnes, agreed to resign from the Rugby Football Union and form their own governing body – the Northern Rugby Football Union.

The issue that prompted the split was professionalism. The stridently amateur RFU, based in London and dominated by southern clubs, objected to the so-called 'broken time' payments that were made to compensate players for time off work. This was a big problem for the predominantly working-class teams from the north, whose players could not afford to forfeit a day's wage. It was a calculatedly anti-working-class rule; many southern players were from public schools. The new Union called their game Rugby League, changing the rules slightly, and it became the normal northern form. Other sports, like tennis, were also dogged by the demand for players to remain amateurs, as were the Olympic Games.

Football was also in the firing line of middle-class respectability, but that had been the case for centuries. Usually involving two groups of players fighting each other to kick something resembling a ball through the doorway of their respective pubs, it had been noisy, violent, destructive of property (and people) and often resulted in magistrates coming down hard on players. It was in Sheffield that a group of men got together to form the first football club. Wanting to attract more players, they invented the first rules of the game, the 'Sheffield Rules'. The game did not at first take off in the rest of Yorkshire – which favoured rugby and thought football a sissy game – until the competitiveness of league football enticed them in. Other teams sprang up.

Sheffield once again was revolutionary when it created the Yorkshire Cricket Club in 1863. Like football, cricket was not particularly popular in the county, but when Yorkshire won the county championships in 1893, people, perhaps for the first time, began to feel pride in the achievements of their county as a whole: they began to identify themselves as Yorkshiremen or women.

EDUCATION

Under the influence of the Evangelical Movement, elementary education had improved during the 1840s and '50s and in 1870 the Elementary Education Act was passed, making it compulsory for boys and girls under the age of 10. Previous to this, reading and writing had been taught in Sunday Schools. There was a lot of opposition from those who worried that if the working classes were taught to 'think' they would become dissatisfied and revolt. One of the driving forces for the Act was the determination to educate the citizens recently enfranchised by the Reform Act to vote wisely. There were also pressures from industrialists who then, as now, feared that Britain's status in the world was being undermined by a lack of education.

Board schools, paid for by the ratepayers, were established across the country, except where some landowners preferred to build their own, perhaps to keep an eye on what was being taught. Secondary education remained too expensive for working-class children until the boards of some industrial towns founded higher-grade schools for promising children. In time the government began to provide grants for technical education, and grammar schools widened their curricula and even began to admit girls.

In 1902 a new Act raised the school leaving age and handed over the board schools to local councils to run. Non-conformist groups who had previously had considerable influence on the old boards were furious, some even refusing to pay their rates. The Act was passed, but it was a disaster for the Conservative government, already unpopular after being in power for years, and they were soundly defeated in the election of 1906.

Self-education was seen as one of the ways out of poverty. Libraries, newspapers, and societies that offered lectures on various subjects from Shakespeare to physics attracted large numbers of people keen to learn new things. In 1903 the Workers' Educational Society was founded to offer adult education to make 'a better world, equal, democratic and just' (Albert Mansbridge, founder).

YORKSHIRE FOLK:

Joseph Wright: Starting in a woollen mill at the age of 6 he taught himself to read and went to night school to learn French and German. He then taught himself Latin and Mathematics, saved enough money to go to Antwerp, walked to Heidelberg University in Germany, studied Sanscrit, Gothic, Old Bulgarian, Lithuanian, Russian, Old Norse, Old and Middle High German, Old Saxon, Old and Middle English, was awarded a doctorate, returned to England, became a professor at Oxford and taught J.R.R. Tolkien philology!

PLACES TO VISIT:

Saltaire Village and Salt's Mill: Shipley, West Yorkshire
Sandygate Road football ground and stadium: 'the oldest ground in the World' according to the *Guinness Book of Records*. Home to Hallam FC
Headingley Cricket Ground: opened in 1891 used for test matches since 1899
The Piece Hall: Blackledge, Halifax, West Yorkshire, HX1 1RE

17

THE TWENTIETH CENTURY

The closer you get to the present day the more events there are for an historian to choose from and the more the streams of Yorkshire's history flow into the national story. I have followed some of those streams as far as I can, but they sometimes just end in a swamp of statistics.

THE FIRST WORLD WAR

On the first two days of public enlistment, 900 men joined the Sheffield City Battalion. Others signed up to the York and Lancaster, the West Yorkshire, the East Yorkshire, the Yorkshire, the Duke of Wellington and the King's Own Yorkshire Light Infantry. A youthful enthusiasm and confidence that the whole thing would be 'over by Christmas' (and that it would be a shame to miss the opportunity) soon led to disillusionment. More men joined the army from the north, Scotland and Ireland than anywhere else in the country, but by 1916 the devastating casualties had blunted

Britain's patriotism to such an extent that conscription had to be introduced.

The factories and mills of Yorkshire were at full stretch for the war effort. Yorkshire women, long used to hard work, took up the slack from the departed men in jobs previously not thought suitable for them. At Armley, Barnbow, Hunslet and Newlay an army of women and girls worked in the new munitions factories. In contrast to the textile mills, great care was taken of the workforce; there were three canteens fitted with the latest equipment; medical care and even dentistry was provided. Despite the greatest caution, however, it was such a dangerous environment that accidents were almost bound to happen. There were explosions – one killed thirty-five women – but such disasters were kept hidden from the general public.

Women were also recruited to Sheffield's east end steelworks, especially the workshops where the shells were produced. The Templeborough Works employed 5,000 women.

The killing of civilians in war had usually been frowned upon, but they became targets for the first time in the Zeppelin raids. Germany's intention was to demoralise

the population, causing Britain to reconsider its position. Zeppelins were not the easiest of things to direct precisely and many bombs fell in open countryside, but English people were unprepared for such 'total war'. Panic spread as the bombs fell, some folk fleeing to the countryside whenever a Zeppelin was spotted. Anti-German feeling increased considerably.

Initially there was no defence because the likelihood of aerial warfare had been discounted by the government. The small fleet of planes that could be scraped together were much slower than the Zeppelins and, anyway, couldn't cover the whole coast, leaving the Germans to raid freely, bombing Hull, Bridlington, Scarborough and other coastal towns before striking further inland towards Leeds and York. They also bombed parts of London and the south coast. Death tolls were low but the intention of demoralising the country had to some extent been achieved.

Eventually the Germans withdrew the Zeppelins, but only because they were vulnerable to the hastily invented and installed anti-aircraft guns and better aeroplanes had been developed.

Immediately following the carnage of the First World War came the carnage of the 1918 Spanish flu pandemic, which killed three times as many people worldwide as the war. A quarter of a million people died in Britain, including Sir Mark Sykes, inheritor of the Sledmere estate. He was famous locally as the founder of the Wolds Wagoners, a group of men trained in handling horses and wagons for moving goods efficiently in war, but has recently become notorious for having been a signatory to the secret Anglo-French Sykes/Picot agreement that divided up the old Ottoman Empire after the war, an important element in the current troubles in the Middle East (fortunately outside the scope of this book). Attempts were made in the early 2000s to get samples from Sir Mark's coffin in the hope of isolating the DNA of the Spanish flu virus, but to no avail.

THE DEPRESSION YEARS

War is an expensive business. The end of the First World War saw Britain's economy slump, just as it had after the Napoleonic Wars. The country had enjoyed the benefit of being the first country in the world to industrialise, now it was going to experience the downside: loss of confidence, an ageing infrastructure, new and well-capitalised competition from other countries. Repercussions continued for the rest of the century.

The post-war slump was bad enough, but then, just as things were beginning to recover in the 1920s, the catastrophic Wall Street Crash produced a world-wide depression. Times became particularly bad in the industrial north as unemployment rose. In some towns like Sheffield the unemployment rate was soon as high as 70 per cent. The Prime Minister realised that ordinary rate payers, themselves hard-pressed, could not be expected to pay for all the poor law relief that was going to be needed. The government therefore decided that a dole should be paid to the unemployed out of national taxation. In order to qualify a worker had to be 'means tested', which meant officials going through every detail of a family's income and savings. People, already humiliated at losing their jobs, felt degraded by the intrusive way in which the testing was done. The memory of this has set the British public against means testing ever since.

Even with the dole many people had to rely on charity and soup kitchens. Levels of childhood diseases, malnutrition and rickets soared. George Orwell's *The Road to Wigan Pier* paints a vivid picture of the time.

Steel production in the north had not kept pace with that of Germany and America though war had given it a temporary boost. Its improved performance could not be maintained in peacetime. Most of the furnaces were small, elderly and family-owned. They needed major investment but there was now no money to invest. Their most important customers, heavy engineering and ship-building companies, also had to reduce their operations in peacetime, with the inevitable knock-on effect on steel manufacturers. Men were thrown out of work all over the country. Soon steel workers made up 34 per cent of Sheffield's unemployed.

There were only two possible solutions open to small steel companies. The first was amalgamation which some chose to do, joining with larger companies to produce huge firms like the United Steel Company and the English Steel Company, which were eventually able to employ thousands of workers. The second solution, preferred by others, was to diversify or specialise in tool steel, high-grade alloys or castings. Steel's unlikely saviour as the Depression came to an end in 1936 was Adolph Hitler, who began to present such a danger that the government decided to re-arm the country. Steel was in demand once again.

Britain's share in the world export of **coal** had fallen considerably since the First World War. This was due to a contracting industry facing a world-wide coal surplus as new coalfields in other countries were opened up.

In 1921 exports and coal prices fell and the mine owners decided to lower the miners' wages. A strike followed, but the miners were forced back to work. Five years later as the Depression deepened the owners proposed not just cutting wages again, but increasing hours as well. The miners were outraged and, led by a Yorkshire miner called Herbert Smith, replied with another strike and the challenging slogan 'Not a penny off the pay. Not a minute on the day!' The Trades Union Congress (TUC) called a general strike in support but the government was ready – particularly alert to possible revolution after the recent one in Russia – and had enlisted middle-class volunteers to maintain essential services. After nine days of strike the TUC gave up. The miners maintained resistance for a few months before being forced to return to work. Many, however, were sacked and remained unemployed for many years. Those still employed were humiliatingly forced to accept longer hours and lower wages.

The bitterness caused by this event both unified and isolated the miners, making them ever more defiant.

Even though the home market was more important than exports to the **textile towns,** they were also hit by the post-war slump because ordinary people had less money to spend on clothes. Unemployment rose steadily in the 1920s, and after the world financial crash, 400 textile firms closed in Halifax alone.

Leeds probably survived the Depression better than other towns because of its diversity. Among the city's other trades was printing, which survived well. Leeds printers produced school and textbooks as well as packs of cards and the new game of Monopoly for Waddington.

The new huge Leeds menswear firm of Montague Burton had spread its financial risks by having shops all over the country, 400 by 1929. Burton, an immigrant Lithuanian Jew, showed what could be achieved in those days by hard work. Starting as a pedlar, he began by selling cheap ready-made suits bought from a dealer, until he had enough money to start his own tailoring business. His story echoes that of Michael Marks, another successful Leeds man, a Jew from Poland, who started a stall in Leeds market with the winning slogan 'Don't ask the price: it's a penny!' He went on to found Marks & Spencer.

HOUSING, 1918–1939

The socialist ideas of the founders of the Fabian Society, Beatrice and Sydney Webb, strongly influenced the members of the 1916 coalition government, and improving the housing stock of working people was high on their list of priorities. No new houses had been built during four years of the war and by 1919 it was obvious that commercial builders had neither the money nor the inclination to build the number of houses that would be needed. The market was not going to provide the 'homes for heroes' that Lloyd George had promised them, but legislation might.

It is hard to emphasise enough what an enormous task this was going to be in Yorkshire. Seventy or eighty years of shoddy back-to-backs built with the scantest of facilities covered thousands of acres of industrial towns in the West Riding. Most were occupied by at least two people to a room, there was one earth closet shared between everyone in the street, and no piped water.

The 1919 Town Planning Act gave councils, for the first time, the right to build domestic houses and compulsorily purchase land. It was followed up in subsequent years by Acts giving them permission to remove slums and force landlords to improve substandard properties. There were also to be schemes of financial assistance. Although there were objections to the whole idea, some councils, particularly in the north, took up the challenge to improve their towns. Hull, Halifax and Bradford councils, where some of the worst slums were, began to build what came to be known as council houses. In Sheffield, over 25,000 houses were demolished under clearance and demolition orders and – at 44 per cent – its rate of replacement was the highest in the country.

By 1933 over a million new homes had been built nationally, though this was still not enough to house all the slum-dwellers. Leeds council had prevaricated and still had 75,000 back-to-backs in the same year. The new Labour chairman of the Housing Committee, the Revd Charles Jenkinson, shocked at the home conditions of some of his congregation, shamed the council into embarking on a massive programme of slum clearance. The new 'garden suburbs' had shops, flats for the elderly and specially designed 'sunshine houses' for the sufferers of the all-too-common consumption. To great opposition, Jenkinson arranged lower rents for lower-paid workers. Fifteen thousand new homes were built in 1937 alone.

Then Jenkinson teamed up with the City Architect, R.A.H. Livett, to build the high-rise Quarry Hill Flats, where 1,000 people were housed in a building so Modernist that Hitler is reputed to have earmarked it for his northern headquarters after the completed conquest of Britain! It had up-to-date features such as electric lighting, a refuse disposal system, and communal amenities such as a shopping parade and a laundry. There was even a swimming pool. What it lacked, of course, was the sense of community that had existed in the squalid back-to-backs, and that, as well as lack of proper maintenance planning, was, in the end, the undoing of so many grand well-intentioned housing schemes in the twentieth century. They were high on theory but low on emotional intelligence.

The first half of the twentieth century, thanks mostly to the actions of local councils, saw huge improvements to ordinary life. Highways, supplies of electricity, water and gas, education, policing, fire services, parks, libraries and art galleries were all improved. The bettering of public health was a particular success; a salaried midwifery service was established under the control of the local authority in the 1930s; health visitors began to be provided to give advice to families, and killer diseases like measles and typhoid were greatly reduced.

LEISURE, 1918–1939

Those who were able to retain their jobs did well in the 1920s and '30s. There was a rise in the standard of living as their housing, diet and health improved. Entertainment undreamed of in previous generations was easily available to city dwellers, and the increase in car ownership meant that even those living in the country could shop or go to the theatre or cinema in their local towns.

Cinema-going was undoubtedly the most popular form of entertainment during this period and even quite small

Yorkshire towns had their own cinema or showed films in village halls. In the larger towns there was plenty of cinematic choice. Hull had thirty cinemas, Leeds sixty-eight, about fifty in Bradford and even York had nine, including the wonderful Electric in Walmgate.

Broadcast radio began in 1921 and the BBC, the first national broadcaster in the world, received its Royal Charter in 1926. By the outbreak of the Second World War most homes had a 'wireless' and listening to it in the evening had become a national practice, even though, to modern taste, some of the programmes seem more like a cure for insomnia. Television was still in its early days and most people would never have seen a broadcast before the Second World War.

Wind-up gramophones had been invented in Victorian times but, minus the great horns, they were still popular, particularly for playing the music of the latest dances, whether the Shimmy and Charleston of the 1920s or the Black Bottom, Foxtrot and Tango of the 1930s. Dancing was still a social skill, a matter of learning the steps, not just doing what you liked. Ballroom dancing was developed during the early part of the century and Jazz gave birth to lots of new dances, though they probably took some time to drift northwards to Yorkshire. Being able to dance was essential because going to a dance was the usual way for young people to meet – parents still liked to keep an eye on their young. There were plenty of local dances, often organised by the church or a local society. Film stars like Fred Astaire and Ginger Rogers were particularly widely admired and emulated.

Sports events attracted very large crowds. The Yorkshire County Cricket Club went on dominating the County Championships and local football teams were by now well supported. Both Huddersfield Town and Sheffield Wednesday did well in the inter-war years. Pay for players was still frowned on and capped at £8 a week (which was actually pretty good at the time when compared with the average wage, though nothing compared with what today's players get).

A fashion for healthy exercise led many who had to be careful of their money to enjoy the countryside with the newly created Ramblers' Association or to stay in cheap Youth Hostels. The Holiday Fellowship opened a centre at Marske in the Dales to provide holidays for the working class. Railways, buses, trams and 'Shanks' pony' (feet) were still the main methods of travel, though charabancs and coaches might be hired for parties or special outings such as Sunday School treats for younger children. Sunday Schools sometimes arranged galas or fêtes in the grounds of big houses, kindly lent by their wealthy owners. These might be attended by hundreds of children, keen to get at the cakes and ice-cream that were an inevitable feature. The church also organised the Whitsun processions of white-clad children and adults led by the local brass band that marked the Whitsun holiday in Yorkshire towns like Sheffield, Goole, Rotherham and Conisbrough.

THE SECOND WORLD WAR

Civilian populations in both England and Germany bore much more of the brunt of the Second World War than they had done in the First. In Yorkshire it was once again coastal cities like Hull which were particularly vulnerable to bombing raids, although bombers now had much longer ranges and could reach targets further inland. This time the government had prepared for aerial attacks by building up the RAF and creating new airfields and aeroplane factories in many places. By the end of the war more than fifty large airfields and operations centres existed across Yorkshire's North, East and West Ridings, from the permanent stations of the 1930s airfields, to satellite bases and substations hastily built to accommodate the vast numbers of allied aircraft. Many of Yorkshire's airfields were home to the

Halifax, Wellington and Whitley squadrons of No. 4 Group RAF, headquartered at RAF Linton-on-Ouse and later Heslington Hall.

Even with the RAF's protection it was not possible to stop German bombing raids entirely: poor Hull suffered eighty-two. The worst came in May 1941 and was so bad that it was said you could read a newspaper in York that night in the red light of Hull's burning. Some 5,000 of Hull's homes and half its central shopping area as well as churches, factories, schools and hospitals were destroyed by the end of the war.

Other towns in Yorkshire, Sheffield and Leeds among them, were targeted, but York, not being an industrial base, might have expected to escape the attentions of the Luftwaffe. Then the RAF bombed Lübeck and, in retaliation, Hitler decided to bomb British cities with particular cultural and historic significance. He chose the sort of places a tourist might find in his Baedeker (a tourist guide), hence the name of these bombings: the Baedeker Raids. Bath, Exeter, Norwich and Canterbury were bombed and on the night of 20 April 1942, York. Missing the minster (in fact, missing *all* the Baedeker minsters) the bombs killed ninety-two people but caused no lasting damage to the city.

NEW CITIZENS

During the war many people from the colonies fought in the British Army or were recruited to fill labour gaps at home. The RAF trained men from the West Indies first as ground crew and later as aircrew. The Merchant Navy would have collapsed had not sailors from all over the colonies worked in the engine rooms. Many of these men died for Britain and at the end of the war there was a feeling that the colonies were owed something.

Britain was now in severe financial trouble. Some towns were seriously damaged and industry needed money for reconstruction. America helped with generous investments but the US also pressed Britain to get rid of its colonies, particularly as some, such as India, were now wanting independence. The Labour government, unexpectedly elected immediately after the war, though wishing to maintain Britain's prestige, was reluctantly pushed into piecemeal decolonisation. Some colonies were disposed of with an almost indecent haste as cheaply as possible, often with little care about their future welfare. The newly independent countries were now renamed the New Commonwealth. Outdated ideas about the greatness of Britain were much harder to get rid of, particularly among those who had fought in the war and thought of themselves as victors.

In the 1950s there was a shortage of labour in worsted-producing towns like Bradford, where the low wages and poor conditions failed to attract ex-soldiers who had been seeing the world or women who had been doing better-paid war work. Word got around and people from the New Commonwealth, able to enter the country freely, and, indeed, actively recruited by the government, were welcomed by mill owners, if only because they were prepared to do the worst jobs for low wages.

The apparent willingness of Britain to welcome them brought more and more immigrants from Pakistan, India, the West Indies and former British colonies in Africa, keen to better their lives. They flocked to the mill towns, where they took on menial jobs and worked unsocial hours, such as the nightshift.

Although Yorkshire people were naturally suspicious of the newcomers, who had to endure plenty of racism, real trouble did not occur until twenty years later, by which time the immigrants had settled, married and produced children. Their numbers had increased to such an extent that in some of the old towns, where they occupied what had been the cheapest districts, whole neighbourhoods had acquired a distinct Asian or Caribbean character. Ethnic groups had always congregated together – the Irish, the Russian Jews and, further back, the Flemish weavers and French glass-workers. The difference was that (except, possibly, for the Irish) they had not gathered in large enough numbers to alarm the indigenous citizens. In actual fact, the number of Commonwealth incomers was very small compared with the population as a whole, but it seemed to some of the original inhabitants that they were being driven out of their own towns by cultures with which they were unfamiliar. Whether justified or not, resentment against people of colour grew, producing on both sides a defensive, inward-looking attitude that has not entirely been eliminated.

Sensing possible danger, the government passed the Commonwealth Immigrants Act in 1962, which restricted immigration from the Commonwealth to those with British passports. Other laws restricting immigration followed, as well as urgently-needed anti-racism legislation.

THE DECLINE OF MANUFACTURING

Nothing remains forever. During the 1960s and '70s many old established firms were forced by foreign competition to either reduce their scale of business or go to the wall. In some cases, this was because of a certain hide-bound inability to accept or contemplate change. This was certainly what happened to the **cloth industry**, which continued to produce sturdy respectable fabrics in restrained colours in the age of Crimplene and the Op-Art mini-skirt. In other cases, it was simply that the cost of replacing outdated machinery was too high.

Added to these problems, Australia began to charge more for its wool, a disaster for the textile mills, most of which were finally finished off by the oil crisis of 1974. Between 1978 and 1981, 16,000 textile jobs were lost in Bradford and the great Victorian mills at Saltaire and Manningham were closed.

Hull's **fishing industry** was reasonably buoyant until 1978, when Iceland imposed a 200-mile exclusion zone around itself, thus barring Hull trawlermen from their richest fishing grounds (though probably saving the cod stocks). The Cod Wars followed, fought by two groups of determined tough men who both saw their way of life threatened. In the end Iceland won because it threatened to withdraw from NATO, thus stopping NATO's access to an important submarine chokepoint. (The Cold War was still ongoing.)

Thousands of fishing jobs were lost in Hull after this, but worse was to follow when the Conservative government under Margaret Thatcher signed up to the EU's Common Fisheries policy in 1983. This allowed all members equal access to each other's waters. By the late 1980s increasingly high prices for fish (once the cheapest of food) had led to Europe-wide over-investment in high-tech boats which could scoop up everything with fins. Stocks of fish, particularly cod, plummeted and led to the imposition of quotas. In the years since then, the number of Hull's fishermen has dropped from 8,000 to almost none, and the fish docks have closed.

The Sheffield **cutlery industry** was fully employed throughout the 1950s and '60s, but the structure of its companies remained basically Victorian and they were soon being undercut by products from the Far East. At the same time, there was a growing glut of Sheffield's other main product, **steel**, as other countries began to produce their own. In this case Yorkshire steelworks had spared no expense in introducing post-war innovations, but a calamitous decline in the demand for steel in the 1970s and '80s resulted in the loss of thousands of jobs. A national steel strike was called in 1981 but it failed, and soon 16.3 per cent of Sheffield's steelworkers were out of work. The same sad story of decline was unfolding in Teesside steelworks.

Desperate attempts were made by councils to keep jobs by re-using redundant steelworks for other purposes. Rotherham's huge Templeborough rolling mill closed in 1998 and was later re-opened as Magna Science Adventure Centre. When Hadfield's Hecla steelworks closed, a new shopping centre was proposed to provide jobs to replace the ones lost, but though Meadowhall employed plenty of people, they were mostly women working part-time for lower wages than a skilled steelworker.

On a more positive note, even though Sheffield's steel output was reduced, it survived and is still of international importance as both it and Rotherham have some of the most advanced steel-melting facilities in the world, making special and stainless steels.

In Sheffield, as in other old manufacturing towns, the largest employers became the service industries in which two-thirds of its workers worked by 2000.

The saddest story of declining industries in Yorkshire is that of **mining**. When the Labour government nationalised the mines in 1946, the National Coal Board took over a workforce of some 700,000 men. Open-cast mining had grown and was by then producing a third of the national output. Smoke from thousands of private houses as well as factories darkened the walls of houses and, particularly in London, combined with other pollutants to produce the deadly smog recorded by Dickens.

All went well with mining until the introduction of imported crude oil began to affect the market. Some of the more uneconomic pits were closed, but the oil crisis of the 1970s improved the bargaining power of the National Union of Mineworkers, which had by then managed to make its members some of the best-paid workers in the country. The Yorkshire miners, with their tough history, were the most militant. They believed that there was an intention on the part of the government to shut down the whole coal industry.

Margaret Thatcher's Conservative government wished to reduce the power of the unions in general, fearing their ability to 'hold the country to ransom'. Industry was turning more and more to oil at the time and coal seemed to have had its day. The closing of more pits would not only save money but reduce union power.

In 1984 a strike was threatened, but since a previous strike had helped to cause the 'three-day week' and the downfall of Conservative Prime Minister Edward Heath, Mrs Thatcher's government prepared carefully, building up ample stocks of coal, and planning to keep as many miners working as possible, even if it meant bringing them in from other pits. Police would be used to stop 'flying pickets' bussed-in from elsewhere to prevent miners working.

When Arthur Scargill, leader of the NUM, called for a strike after the closing of various pits, miners at Cortonwood Colliery near Rotherham walked out in response. However, Scargill, fatally, failed to call for a strike ballot as demanded by law. The strike was thus deemed illegal, but it continued, with skirmishes between the police and the 'flying pickets'. The worst of these was 'the Battle of Orgreave', where 500 miners confronted a similar number of police on horses. On television it looked curiously like a medieval battle between knights and peasants, and it has certainly been mythologised as such, but, in fact, more policemen than miners were injured. The failure of the NUM to hold the strike ballot alienated many of the other unions.

In the end the strike failed but not before the Union itself split. The government had won. Afterwards, the fears of the miners were justified as most of the Yorkshire pits were closed, their communities damaged, unemployed and divided. Now, as the grass and trees cover the black spoil heaps, a visitor might never know that collieries had ever been there.

NEW DEVELOPMENTS

Despite the disappearance of old industries, national standards of living rose during the last half of the twentieth century, even in the devastated West Riding. There was a general feeling of optimism in the country during the 1950s: young people were having babies and planning new lives.

Food rationing continued for a while but clothing rationing was over and women could flaunt Dior's full New Look
skirts. Not many Yorkshire people could afford to go to
the Festival of Britain in London, but they were treated to a
glimpse of its delights when the Festival Touring Exhibition
came to Leeds.

The enthusiastic Labour government that took power
after the war was determined to carry out its theories of
nationalisation. Mining and the railways were among the
industries that became public property in this way. On
5 July 1948, the National Insurance Act, National Assistance
Act and National Health Service Act came into force, form-
ing the key planks of the modern UK Welfare State.

Other Acts improved the environment. An almost
magical change came about when the 1956 Clean Air Act
was passed, probably doing more to improve the health
of city dwellers than almost anything else, while the Town
and Country Act gave local authorities power that they had
never had before to improve the life of their citizens. They
were also given the money to do it with (though for some
councillors, later disgraced, this proved to be a temptation
too far). Slums were cleared, greenbelts designated, and, as
car ownership increased, new roads, bypasses and multi-
storey carparks built.

Sheffield, no longer 'the foulest town in England', became
the cleanest industrial city in Western Europe, though
housing continued to be a problem, somewhat eased by the
high-rise blocks of flats constructed at Park Hill and Hyde
Park. Ironically, they were inspired by Quarry Hill, which
was about to be demolished. They dominated the east side
of the city, 'streets in the sky'. Always subjects of debate,
some have been demolished and there is now a plan for their
redevelopment, though some residents still value them.

Not everything achieved by the Town and Country Act
was good. Fearing to seem old-fashioned, some councils
swept away much of the historic centre of their towns,
replacing them with bland concrete and glass blocks

lacking any local connection or character. Bradford, in particular, destroyed some of its finest Victorian buildings. Perhaps one of the biggest changes in the look of the county was the expansion of suburbs into the countryside. Most towns were forced to allow this in order to make room for rehousing slum dwellers and to accommodate their ever-growing populations.

Up until the 1960s a series of terrible decisions were made by councils with large numbers of poor people to send many of their 'surplus' children out of the country to be brought up in Australia or Canada. It was done, rather quietly, to reduce welfare costs. Most of the children sent from Yorkshire went from Hull, Leeds and other West Riding towns. It is unlikely that any of the councils and organisations involved had any idea of the horrible child abuse many of these children would have to endure, and which has only recently been revealed, but it was an action of often appalling cruelty for which a belated national apology has been made.

Council tenants were given the right to buy their council houses by Margaret Thatcher's government, thus removing huge numbers from the council's rental lists while free-ing councils (and ratepayers) from the enormous ongoing expense of maintaining them. The belief was that business would step in and build more, but, sadly, this did not happen, builders preferring to build more expensive houses, especially as the cost of building land rose.

Sometimes during this period, it seemed that cars were more important than their owners: new ring roads and flyovers made life for pedestrians difficult, noisy and dirty. York's proposed inner ring road, which would have removed whole streets of Georgian houses, was rejected by the inhabitants, even though planning permission had been given, which is one of the reason its tourist industry flourishes. The West Riding towns were not so lucky.

The nationalisation of the railways was a mixed blessing because government attention was drawn to the uneconomic nature of many of its lines. The general love affair with cars convinced many in power that the days of railways were numbered, short-sightedly failing to see how congested roads would soon become. The first chairman of the recently privatised British Railways Board, Dr Richard Beeching, was asked by Harold MacMillan's Conservative government to report on the state of Britain's railways and suggest where cuts might be made. His report was accepted and the size of the network reduced ruthlessly by a third. Unfortunately, once a railway disappeared it was far too expensive to repurchase the land and rebuild it when, in later years, it became apparent that the cuts had been too draconian. The railways were subsequently re-privatised under John Major's government in 1993.

Many Yorkshire people were upset by the Local Government Act of 1972. Under the Act, the Ridings lost their lieutenancies and shrievalties, while the administrative counties, county boroughs and their councils were abolished. Yorkshire was now divided between a number of metropolitan and non-metropolitan counties. Some new counties incorporated parts of old counties: Cleveland, for example, was created out of part of the North Riding and Teesside, while Humberside incorporated Hull and most of the East Riding, as well as taking Goole from the West Riding. South Yorkshire (there was never a South Riding historically) took territory from the West Riding. Other equally disruptive changes were made in other areas. The worst aspect of this change was the disappearance of the time-honoured Ridings. There was serious opposition in some areas, particularly over the creation of Humberside. The Borough of Beverley changed its name to the East Yorkshire Borough of Beverley in protest. In the 1990s, popular opinion had some success: Cleveland and Humberside were both abolished. Cleveland became part of the North Riding and the East Riding was reinstated.

Service industries continued to grow as new universities opened at York, Bradford, Sheffield Hallam, Huddersfield and Hull. The Halifax Building Society opened its headquarters in Halifax in 1973 and by the 1990s was the largest employer in Calderdale. In Leeds there was a rapid growth of accountancy and law firms. Tourism increased during the last decades of the century, eventually becoming a significant contributor to the county's economy. This success was partly due to the beauty of the Yorkshire countryside and partly because of its huge number of historic buildings and museums. The Jorvik Centre, opened in 1984, introduced thousands of people to York's Viking heritage. Across the county museums and attractions opened to bring in income to towns with little other employment.

Though most of the old wartime airfields had gone, some were retained and turned into international airports. RAF Finningley became Doncaster Sheffield Airport, RAF Kirmington became Humberside Airport. Most successful of all was an airfield where once 700 Lancaster bombers were made: it was transformed into Leeds-Bradford Airport. Now Yorkshire folk could travel more easily to those holidays in foreign parts that had become the norm by the millennium.

THE COUNTRYSIDE

By the end of the twentieth century, life in Yorkshire's rural villages had been made much easier with electricity and other services, TV, radio and particularly telephones. Cars, a blessing and essential in some ways, proved a curse in others as rural people abandoned local shops in favour of the larger variety in town. Village shops, post offices and small businesses closed up and down the county.

Rural schools hung on, though some parents worried about their children's social integration, preferring to drive them to larger schools in nearby towns. This, together with the downturn of the birth rate, forced some to close for lack of pupils.

Horses were still used on many small farms until the 1960s, but by then mechanisation was taking over a lot of the work and jobs were being lost from the land. Dilapidated country cottages, no longer needed for workers, could be bought for very little, inspiring people looking for holiday homes to buy them up. In places like the Moors and Dales, large numbers of houses were lost to the local market over the last decades of the century as prices inexorably rose, but new residents who intended to spend a reasonable amount of time in a village, even the dreaded 'Southerner', were usually welcomed as they often brought energy, custom and ideas with them.

In 2000 the upland parts of Yorkshire were still farmed in much the same way as they always had been, albeit with fewer labourers and more machinery. Subsidies from the European Union brought money for farm roads and improved equipment (as well as imposing unwelcome bureaucracy). Hill farmers came to rely on subsidies to keep their farms going; however, just like their ancestors, they often had to take second jobs to earn a sufficient living.

In lowland villages the mixed farming of livestock and arable continued as before but with more emphasis on cash crops such as potatoes, sugar beet and carrots. Oilseed rape received generous subsidies and was soon making the spring fields brilliant. Occasional fields of borage or flax sprang up as farmers tried out different crops. In Holderness about 60 per cent of the land remained arable, much of it, particularly around Sunk Island, valuable Crown land.

The interference of government in farming was a relatively new but increasing thing, begun during the Second World War. Our entry into Europe only increased this tendency. The use of pesticides and artificial fertilisers was encouraged after the war as pressure to grow more food increased. It was a successful policy but by the end of the century the long-term effects of their use were becoming better understood and they were increasingly coming under attack. The agricultural policies introduced by the European

Union were intended to improve food quality and animal welfare, in which they were more or less successful, but some of its other subsidies unintentionally led to practices that severely affect biodiversity and soil health.

Another legacy of the post-war Labour government was the passing of an Act to establish National Parks. By the end of the 1950s the Yorkshire Dales, the North Yorkshire Moors and the Peak District (some of which is in Yorkshire) were on the list. These three parks, together with the National Trust, worked hard to preserve traditional landscapes. Tourism in Yorkshire, particularly the countryside, continued to grow throughout the last part of the century and visitor centres – often accompanied by a tearoom – were opened to inform and educate the visitors. The traditional outdoor activities of walking and climbing were joined by the less strenuous one of visiting the rural locations of television series. The books of James Herriot, televised as *All Creatures Great and Small*, brought visitors to Thirsk, the location of the original veterinary practice, while others went to Holmfirth, the filming site of *Last of the Summer Wine* or Goathland, the village where *Heartbeat* was set. The Brontë's Haworth (its rear adorned with a huge shop that would be shocking to its former owners) remained as popular as ever.

Old country pastimes such as hunting, shooting (both clay and pheasant), riding and racing continued (the oldest horserace in England is still held at Kiplingcotes in the Wolds) as well as the new activities of mountain-biking and orienteering. Villagers, many now ageing, gave up dances at the village hall in favour of whist, beetle drives and car boot sales. The shared communal pleasures of harvest or carol singing began to fade from public memory.

YORKSHIRE FOLK:
Alan Bennett (b. 9 May 1934) is a Leeds-born play-wright, author, screenwriter and actor. He studied history at Oxford, where he performed with the Oxford Revue, and subsequently remained there researching mediaeval history and teaching for a while. A collaboration with Dudley Moore, Peter Cook and Jonathan Miller resulted in the wildly successful *Beyond the Fringe* revue at the 1960 Edinburgh Festival which brought them all instant fame. After this Alan was able to give up his academic work and become a full-time writer. His first play, *Forty Years On*, produced in 1968, was his first stage play, and his later work includes the *Talking Heads* monologues and the scripts and screen adaptations for *The Madness of King George* and *The History Boys*.

PLACES TO VISIT:
National Railway Museum: est. 1975, Leeman Road, York
Sheffield Winter Gardens: 90 Surrey Street, Sheffield, South Yorkshire, S1 2LH
Yorkshire Sculpture Park: West Bretton, Wakefield, West Yorkshire, WF4 4LG

AFTERWORD

History, of course, does not stop with the year 2000, but the history of Yorkshire is now more than ever merged into that of Britain, just as that of Britain is merged with bigger world concerns. It may be that one day the history of the obscure inhabitants of a particular acreage of land in an obscure northern part of a small and obscure northern county will no longer be of interest to anyone, except to you, of course.

If, like me, you are an incomer (or a visitor) then I hope this book will help you understand and appreciate the place you now call home a little more; if, on the other hand, you are Yorkshire born and bred, then this is your own history and the tough, intractable, kindly, indefatigable people of 'God's own county' are your own ancestors. Remember their stories, honour and be proud of them!

INDEX